Who Murdered Yitzhak Rabin?

Who Murdered Yitzhak Rabin?

Barry Chamish

FERAL HOUSE

Further material by Barry Chamish
regarding Rabin's murder can be
accessed at the following website:
www.webseers.com/rabin

Who Murdered Yitzhak Rabin? ©1998 Barry Chamish

ISBN 0-922915-50-4

Feral House
2532 Lincoln Blvd. Suite 359
Venice, CA 90291

The publisher wishes to thank Robert Sterling of www.konformist.com
for calling Feral House's attention to Barry Chamish's research, and
Jessica Peabody for her welcome editorial assisstance.

Design by Linda Hayashi

10 9 8 7 6 5 4 3 2 1

Yitzhak Rabin
was murdered on
November 4, 1995.

ACKNOWLEDGEMENTS

There are many people in Israel who want the truth of the Rabin assassination smothered and fewer who want it exposed. The latter have endured much public and professional wrath for their courage and I thank them all for their inner strength.

My choice of an inexperienced researcher, Yechiel Mann was entirely justified by his discoveries. As usual, Joel Bainerman provided inspired perspective. Natan Gefen and Marc Weiss provided solid investigatory proofs. Brian Bunn organized a famous lecture that exposed my work to a national audience. I am forever grateful for his courage, as I am to all who invited me to address their organizations. Journalists Avi Segal, Emma Sodnikov and Zeev Barcella are the bravest and best; they were the first in Israel to conclude I may be right and wrote so in lengthy articles. I am forever grateful to Evgenia Kravchick for skillfully translating my work for a widespread Russian-language readership. Jay Bushinsky and his partner Linda Amar of NBC-Extra were the first correspondents from a popular foreign media who understood the strength of my case and had the integrity to let America know. Eli Wohlgelernter is to be commended for his balanced front page report in the usually timid *Jerusalem Post*. Professor Arieh Zaretski is the person I credit most for having my work accepted by so many in academia.

By the end of 1997, numerous Israeli journalists finally stuck their necks out and risking the mockery of their peers, examined the facts objectively. They include Prof. Hillel Weiss, Adir Zik, Dr. Joel Cohen, Gadi Blum, Shimon Zilber, Hagai Huberman, Baruch Gordon, Hagai Segal, Ram Ezrach, and Melech Klosner. The previous journalists are mostly religious or politically conservative. Yuval Yoaz deserves special mention because he gave me a fair shake in Anashim, a magazine which appeals to the constituency in Israel which does not want to believe it could have happened.

Finally, there are about fifty people who provided me with essential information but would not want to be acknowledged by name. You know who you are. You know how much your information meant to me by the contents of this book.

CONTENTS

INTRODUCTION

There are successful assassinations where the murderers never get caught. The conspiracy to murder Yitzhak Rabin shouldn't be one of them. It was a sloppy conspiracy and the murderers could eventually be brought to justice. But, for a variety of reasons, the Israeli political establishment is ignoring many indisputable clues to avoid pursuing justice.

Yitzhak Rabin was an ideal target for assassination. As Prime Minister, a peace process with the PLO and Syria was forced upon him from abroad. He became a willing advocate of a diplomacy which was leading to Israel's sure demise. He faced mortal danger from two opposing camps: the minions of Israelis who fought the peace process; and the foreign and Israeli powerbrokers who supported it. The former was blamed for the murder while the latter was responsible for it.

This book does not, however, delve into Rabin's murky diplomatic ties nor does it name who gave the order for the assassination. No one knows who was at the top of the conspiracy. But, the reader will discover who had to have been involved at the operational level, and learn just as surely that Rabin could not have possibly been killed by his accused murderer, Yigal Amir.

To keep the peace process on track, it was vital that all opponents be discredited. Opposition came from all quarters in Israel, even from within Rabin's Labour Party. (One faction of which eventually broke off to join the later Likud-led government.) Typical of the most vocal opponents, Yigal Amir was religious, right-wing and Sephardi. He was the most politically useful patsy that could be devised.

Yigal Amir was an activist of the supposed anti-peace process organization, Eyal (acronym for the Organization of Jewish Warriors). Eyal, however, was a front created by the General Security Services (Shabak, Israel's FBI), helmed by Avishai Raviv, a Shabak agent since 1987. As part of a covert operation assigned to attract anti-peace process radicals to Eyal and set them up for arrest. Ample testimony has been gathered from people who witnessed his methods. Herein it will be made clear that one of his duties was to provoke Yigal Amir into shooting Rabin.

Many, if not most of the Shabak agents, and possibly several policeman on duty the night of the assassination, were instructed to allow a sting operation to take place. Yigal Amir would be provided with a gun loaded with blanks. He would shoot at Rabin and be caught red-handed. Rabin's government would then have the justification to order a nation-wide crackdown on opponents of the peace process.

And indeed, after Rabin was shot, Shabak agents yelled, "They're blanks," "It was a toy gun," "It's an exercise," "They were caps," "It wasn't real," "Dummy bullets," and the like because they thought the sting had taken place.

But there was a double-cross. Amir shot his blank bullets and Rabin, very much alive, was shoved into his limousine where the real assassin lay in wait. What should have been a one minute trip to the hospital took over eight minutes meandering down the dark streets of Tel Aviv. During that time, the murderer completed his job and left the car.

This is neither speculation nor theory. The author has collected hundreds of pages of police reports, court protocols, and public and personal testimony enough to demonstrate the veracity of these conclusions.

Just a few of the clues the conspirators left behind include:

- The amateur film of the assassination showing the back door of Rabin's "empty" limosine being slammed shut before he enters the vehicle.
- The same film documenting that Rabin's bodyguards allowed Amir to take a clear shot at the Prime Minister and that he survived it.
- Testimony from witnesses a few feet from Rabin, including his wife, who saw him continue walking briskly after being shot. Ten minutes after the "shooting," one witness, Miriam Oren, told a national television audience, "Rabin wasn't hurt. I saw him walk into the car."
- Testimony from numerous security and police officers who did not believe Rabin was shot because he didn't fall, cry out in pain, or bleed.
- Police laboratory tests concluding that Rabin was shot point

blank, though the government's commission of inquiry concluded that Amir shot from a good half meter's distance.

• The Police ballistics report stating that Amir's clip contained
only eight bullets, though he loaded nine.

• The unexplainable disappearance of the bullets for 11 hours
after their supposed removal from Rabin's body.

• The death certificate signed by Dr. Mordecai Gutman, one of
the surgeons who operated on Rabin, stating that he was shot
through the chest from the front and that his spine was shattered, claims backed the same evening by an operating room
nurse, the Health Minister, the Director of Ichilov Hospital, a
patient and even Foreign Minister Shimon Peres. The official
version of events has Amir shooting Rabin in the back with no
spinal damage.

The conspiracy was so bungled that not only was abundant physical evidence left behind, but the conspirators themselves didn't
coordinate their testimony with one another, and ended up contra-
dicting each other at every opportunity.

It would have been so simple if an aggrieved radical had actually
assassinated Rabin. But Amir's deep ties to the very people who were
charged with protecting the Prime Minister, begins to demonstrate
the web of deceit and criminality perpetrated by the Shabak.

Amir and Rabin were not the only victims. There were many others, both Jew and Arab. We can only hope that this book will help
see that they were the last.

Chapter One
THE CONSPIRACY EMERGES

It took almost two years after the Kennedy assassination for the American public to begin to suspect a conspiracy. It took less than two weeks before suspicions arose among many Israelis that Rabin may not have been murdered by a lone gunman.

The first to propose this possibility, on November 11, one week following the assassination, was Professor Michael Hersiger, a Tel Aviv University historian. He told the Israeli press, "There is no rational explanation for the Rabin assassination. There is no explaining the breakdown. In my opinion there was a conspiracy involving the Shabak. It turns out the murderer was in the Shabak when he went to Riga. He was given documents that permitted him to buy a gun. He was still connected to the Shabak at the time of the murder."

Hersiger's instincts were right, but he believed the conspirators were from a right-wing rogue group in the Shabak. It wasn't long before suspicions switched to the left. On the 16th of November, a territorial leader and current Knesset Member, Benny Eilon, called a press conference during which he announced, "There is a strong suspicion that Eyal and Avishai Raviv not only were connected loosely to the Shabak but worked directly for the Shabak. This group incited the murder. I insist that not only did the Shabak know about Eyal, it founded and funded the group."

The public reaction was sceptical. Yet Eilon turned out to be right on the money. How did he know ahead of everyone else?

Film director Merav Ktorza and her cameraman Alon Eilat interviewed Eilon in January, 1996. Off camera he told them, "Yitzhak Shamir called me into his office a month before the assassination and told me, 'They're planning to do another Arlosorov on us. [In 1933, left wing leader Chaim Arlosorov was murdered in Tel Aviv, and the right-wing Revisionists were falsely blamed for it. This was Israel's first political murder and its repercussions were extensive.] Last time they did it, we didn't get into power for fifty years. I want you to identify anyone you hear of threatening to murder Rabin and stop him.'"

Shamir was the former head of the Mossad's European desk and had extensive intelligence ties. Two witnesses heard Eilon make the remarkable claim that Shamir was informed of the impending assassination in October, 1995; Eilon, however, would not appear on camera with it or any other statement. Shortly after his press conference and testimony to the Shamgar Commission, Eilon stopped talking publicly about the assassination.

There are two theories about his sudden shyness. Shmuel Cytryn, the Hebron resident, who was jailed without charge two months before the assassination, after identifying Raviv as a Shabak agent, has hinted that Eilon played some role in the Raviv affair, and that he was covering his tracks at the press conference.

Many others believe that pressure was applied on Eilon using legal threats against his niece Margalit Har Shefi. Because of her acquaintance with Amir, she was charged as an accessory to the assassination. To back up their threats, the Shabak had Amir write a rambling, incriminating letter to her from prison. The fear of his niece spending a decade in jail might have been enough to put a clamp down on Eilon.

Public opinion of Eilon's claims changed the following evening when journalist Amnon Abramovitch announced on national television the discovery that the leader of Eyal, Yigal Amir's good friend Avishai Raviv, was in fact a Shabak agent code-named "Champagne" for the bubbles of incitement he raised.

The announcement caused a national uproar. The major Israeli newspaper *Maariv* wrote: "Amnon Abramovitch dropped a bombshell last night.... Now we ask the question, why didn't he [Avishai Raviv] report Yigal Amir's plan to murder Rabin to his superiors? In conversations with security officials, the following picture emerged. Eyal was under close supervision by the Shabak. They supported it monetarily for the past two years. The Shabak knew the names of all Eyal members, including Yigal Amir."

That same day, November 16, 1995, the newspaper *Yediot Ahronot* reported details of a crime that would not go away. "There is a version of the Rabin assassination that includes a deep conspiracy within the Shabak. The Raviv affair is the cornerstone of the conspiracy plan.

"Yesterday, a story spread among the settlers that Amir was supposed to fire a blank bullet, but that he knew he was being set up, so he replaced the blanks with real bullets. The story explains why after the shooting, the bodyguards shouted that 'the bullets were blanks.'

The story sounds fantastic but the Shabak's silence is fueling it."

Abramovitch's scoop established a direct sinister connection between the murderer and the people protecting the Prime Minister. But who was responsible for the leak? There are two candidates who were deeply involved in the protection of Eyal but probably knew nothing of its plans to murder Rabin. They are then Police Minister Moshe Shahal and then Attorney General Michael Ben Yair.

Shahal was asked for his reaction to the Abramovitch annoucement. He said simply, "Amnon Abramovitch is a very reliable journalist," by ommision verifing the Champagne story.

Shahal's knowledge of Raviv's true identity is further evidenced by revelations in the Israeli press.

Maariv, November, 24, 1995
The police issued numerous warrants against Avishai Raviv but he was never arrested. There was never a search of his home.

Kol Ha Ir, January, 1996
Nati Levy: "It occurs to me in retrospect that I was arrested on numerous occasions but Raviv, not once. There was a youth from Shiloh who was arrested for burning a car. He told the police that he did it on Raviv's orders. Raviv was held and released the same day."

Yediot Ahronot, May 12, 1995
When they aren't involved in swearing-in ceremonies, Eyal members relax in an apartment in Kiryat Araba, near the home of the Baruch Goldstein's family. [Baruch Goldstein, murderer of 29 Arabs in the Hebron massacre of March 1994.] And yet, the police have been unsuccessfully searching for the apartment for some time.

Everyone in the neighborhood, as well as the media knew the Eyal apartment was in the same building as Goldstein's. But, the police left it alone because Raviv used it for surveillance.

He was immune to arrest for such "minor" crimes as arson and threats of murder to Jews and Arabs alike. But police inaction was most inexcusable in two well-publicized incidents.

Yerushalayim, November 10, 1995
Eyal activists have been meeting with Hamas and Islamic
Jihad members to plan joint operations.

This item was reported throughout the country, but Avishai
Raviv was not arrested for treason, terrorism and cavorting with the
enemy. Less explicable yet was the police reaction to Raviv taking
responsibility, "credit" as he called it, for the murder of three
Palestinians in the town of Halhoul.

On December 11, 1993, three Arabs were killed by men wearing
Israeli army uniforms. Eyal called the media the next day claiming
the slaughter was its work. But Moshe Shahal did not order the arrest
of Eyal members. He knew Eyal wasn't responsible. He knew they
only took responsibility to blacken the name of West Bank settlers.
His only action, according to *Globes,* December 13, 1993, was to tell
"… the cabinet that heightened action was being taken to find the
killers and to withdraw the legal rights of the guilty organization."

After a week of international condemnation of the settlers, the
army arrested the real murderers, four Arabs from the town.

At that point Shahal should have had Raviv arrested for issuing
the false proclamation on behalf of Eyal. But Shahal did not. This
inaction can only be explained if he were ordered not to interfere
with this Shabak operation.

Also under orders was Attorney-General Michael Ben Yair who
was so terrified of possible revelations at the Shamgar Commission
that he sat in on every session on behalf of the government. Later
he, along with Prime Minister Peres, approved the sections to be
hidden from the public.

After the assassination, it emerged that two left wing Knesset
members had previously submitted complaints against Eyal to Ben
Yair. On March 5, 1995 Dedi Tzuker asked Ben Yair to investigate
Eyal after it distributed inciteful literature at a Jerusalem high
school. And on September 24, 1995, Yael Dayan requested that Ben
Yair open an investigation of Eyal in the wake of its televised vow to
spill the blood of Jews and Arabs who stood in the way of their
goals. He ignored both petitions, later explaining, "Those requests
should have been submitted to the army or the Defense Minister
[Yitzhak Rabin]."

Both Shahal and Ben Yair were probably ordered to cover-up Eyal's incitements. But when one incitement turned out to be the murder of Rabin, one of them panicked and decided to place all the blame on the Shabak.

Which one?

According to Abramovitch, "I have a legal background so my source was a high-ranking legal official." He could be suggesting Ben Yair ... which hardly exonerates him or Shahal. Supplying Eyal with immunity from arrest or prosecution, enabled the assassination of Yitzhak Rabin.

As late as June, 1997, Ben Yair opened a police complaint against the "Deep Throat," and reporter Abramovich was summoned to give evidence—all implying the leak came from a "traitor" in Ben Yair's office. Whether the leak actually came from one of these men, a great unlikelihood, or just someone from their offices, his willingness to reveal the truth has laid a foundation on which this conspiracy could be laid bare.

Chapter Two
PROVOKING AMIR INTO MURDER

Numerous witnesses verify seeing and hearing Shabak agent Avishai Raviv provoking Yigal Amir into assassinating Yitzhak Rabin. Concentrating his efforts on Amir, rather than any other Eyal activist, Raviv utilized a long campaign of psychological pressure.

For reasons known to Shabak, a group practiced in psychological warfare, Amir was well-chosen for his job. Not many people are capable of murder even if prodded relentlessly. Somehow, Raviv knew Amir was a fit candidate for the job.

Yigal Amir spent the spring and summer of 1992 in Riga, Latvia on assignment from the Liaison Department of the Prime Minister's Office, usually called Nativ. In one of the greater ironies of the assassination drama, it was Prime Minister Rabin who was ultimately responsible for assigning Amir to the Riga post.

There is an even greater irony to the assassination tale. Acting on State Comptroller reports of massive financial corruption, Rabin was preparing to shut down Nativ. Some have considered this a motive for the murder. An early, and false, excuse of the Shabak to explain how Amir was let into the sterile area was that he presented government credentials in the form of his Nativ identity card.

Nativ was and is a nest of spies. Originally founded in the early 1950s as a liaison between Israel and Jews trapped behind the Iron Curtain, over the years, according to major Israel newspaper *Haaretz,* November, 1995, "It had developed its own independent intelligence and operational agenda."

Some evidence of these claims was revealed in June, 1996, when the Russian government arrested and then expelled a Nativ worker named Daniel for illegally acquiring classified satellite photos. Indignant, the Russians threatened to close all of Israel's immigration offices in the country. The indignation was renewed in January, 1997, when Daniel was appointed Nativ's head of intelligence.

Another source of Russian indignation is the fact that Nativ has been granting visas to Israel for major criminals including members of the Russian mafia and a former president of the Ukraine who escaped to Tel Aviv with $30 million stolen from his country's treasury. The escape occurred barely five months after meeting with Police Minister Moshe Shahal and Foreign Minister Shimon Peres in Kiev.

Within days of the assassination, the government went on full-tilt to explain away Amir's Riga sojourn. The government did admit that Amir was a Hebrew teacher for five months there. But since he had no teacher's degree nor spoke Latvian, the story wasn't accepted. So Police Minister Moshe Shahal explained that Amir was a security guard for only three months in Riga.

The government clearly didn't like Amir's Shabak ties speculated upon, so Aliza Goren, the spokeswoman for the Prime Minister's Office told reporters, "Amir was never in Riga and anyone who reports that he was is being totally irresponsible."

That ploy fell to bits when the BBC's *Panorama* program interviewed Amir's family and filmed his passport. Stamped within was a bold CCCP. Goren had lied and by implication was guilty of covering up a fact that the government clearly did not want revealed.

Speculation was widespread by the beginning of 1996 that Amir was on an intelligence mission on behalf of the Prime Minister's Office in Riga. Israel Television's Channel One broadcast a long interview with Moshe Levanon, the former head of Nativ. He insisted that his organization had no intelligence ties and then presented a series of photos illustrating his work. Included was one of him standing with former CIA Director George Bush, apparently in Russia.

Whatever Amir's true purpose in Riga, the mild-mannered soldier returned in the fall of 1992 with a changed personality. Something happened there to alter his mindset. He was now Amir, the campus radical of Bar Ilan University. But whatever it was, Amir was not yet a murderer, Avishai Raviv had his job cut out to exploit Amir's psychological weaknesses and transform him into a political assassin.

Maariv, November 9, 1996
"It was said amongst us that Rabin was a persecutor and could be sentenced to die according to biblical precepts," related Avishai Raviv at his hearing yesterday.

Maariv, November 10, 1995
An Eyal poster on Bar Ilan campus showed a photo of Rabin covered in blood. Interested students were asked to phone Raviv's beeper number for more information.

Maariv, December 12, 1995
"Several times I heard from Yigal Amir that he intended to hurt the Prime Minister but I didn't take it seriously," Avishai Raviv testified to the Shamgar Commission.

Behind closed doors, Raviv testified that he once had a discussion with Amir about bullets for the gun. One implication of this testimony is that Raviv may have supplied Amir with what he thought were blank bullets.

Maariv, November 24, 1995
According to Sarah Eliash, a schoolteacher working at the Shomron Girls Seminary, some of her pupils heard Raviv encourage Amir to murder Rabin. He told him, "Show us you're a man. Do it."

Yediot Ahronot, December 11, 1995
One of the pupils said Raviv called a few government members "monsters" and added that it was necessary to blow up the whole government to get rid of the "persecutors."

Another pupil told how Raviv used quotes from biblical commentary to prove the need to kill Rabin ...

Uri Dan and Dennis Eisenberg,* writing for the *Jerusalem Post*, elaborated on the girls' later testimony behind closed doors at the Shamgar Commission:

> Sarah Eliash had already appeared voluntarily before the commission and related how her pupils had run to see her on the night of the killing. In tears they said they knew Yigal Amir.
>
> They had met both Amir and Avishai Raviv, the GSS agent, at the settlement of Barkan last summer ...
>
> "We used to see Raviv and Amir on Saturdays during last summer," they related. "These gatherings were arranged by Yigal—Raviv was real macho. He kept saying to Yigal: 'You keep talking about killing Rabin. Why don't you do it? Are you frightened? You say you want to do it. Show us that you're a man. Show us what you're made of.'"
>
> The other girls present corroborated the evidence. How did Amir react to the goading by Raviv? All replied in roughly the same way: "He didn't react. He just sat there and said nothing or changed the subject."

Geula Amir, Yigal's mother, "writes" in the February 1997 *George* magazine (her piece was actually ghostwritten by two Jerusalem-based journalists):

> According to Yigal's friends and others who have since testified in court, Raviv seemed to be obsessed with one topic: killing Rabin. He and Yigal frequently engaged in discussions about the feasibility of the assassination ...
>
> Several young women said that they recognized Yigal and Raviv from a Sabbath retreat. The girls told their teacher Sarah Eliash that Raviv had denounced several Rabin government officials as "traitors." During several marathon ideological dis-

---

* Authors of *A State Crime—The Assassination of Yitzhak Rabin* published in France in 1996.

cussions that weekend, Raviv had attempted to goad Yigal into killing Rabin, ridiculing his cowardice for not being willing to kill a "traitor."

Eran Agelbo, testifying as a witness for the defense at Yigal's trial, revealed that Raviv had said that Rabin was a *rodef*—the Hebrew term for someone who endangers others and therefore should be killed—Agelbo also maintained that Raviv had verbally pressured Yigal to attempt an assassination of Rabin.

"Raviv told Yigal and others that there was a judgement on Yitzhak Rabin. He said, 'Rabin should die and whoever killed him would be a righteous person.' Raviv had a powerful influence on Yigal. He continuously emphasized to him and other students that whoever implemented the judgement against Rabin was carrying out a holy mission."

Nice talk from a Shabak agent, and so much for Raviv and other Shabak officers' claims that Amir came up with the idea to kill Rabin all by himself. To acquire original testimony I phoned one of Sarah Eliash's pupils. She began talking to me in Hebrew, but the phone was taken from her by her American-born father. A twenty-minute discussion took place, extracts of which follow:

"____ is not willing to talk to you, do you understand? She has nothing to say."

"We'll never get to the truth if she doesn't."

"Find someone else if you can. I'm not willing to let anything happen to my daughter. You have to understand that, don't you? You don't know what's going on. They promised her if she testified that nothing would happen afterward; no arrests or threats. They lied. She can't talk to you and that's that."

"What about her civil duty? What kind of a country will it be if everyone lets criminals off?"

"I used to think like that. This is no democracy. You don't know what it is. When I came here I thought it was to be free as a Jew. Now I just want to avoid getting in trouble. I can't tell you what they said they'd do to her if she talked anymore."

In total, over a dozen people testified to seeing Raviv prod Amir into killing Rabin. But that was not the sum total of his involvement.

Eyal member, Arieh Oranj, told me: "Our plan was to go to Gaza to participate in another demonstration to counterbalance the one in Tel Aviv. But at the last minute Raviv changed his mind and led us to the Tel Aviv rally. Not two minutes after the shooting, Raviv told us, 'Do you know who did it? Yigal Amir.'"

Maariv, November 10, 1995

Last Saturday night, minutes after Prime Minister Rabin was shot and well before the killer was identified, Avishai Raviv, head of Eyal, already announced that the assassin was Yigal Amir.

Immediately after the shooting, several reporters received messages on their pagers proclaiming that "Eyal takes responsibility for the deed." A *Maariv* reporter quickly called Raviv who denied responsibility for the shooting, saying, "We have no connection to this act. This is not our type of operation." But he did give out information about Yigal Amir, his name, that he was a student at Bar Ilan, and his army records.

Minutes after the shooting, an unknown group called "Jewish Vengeance" called dozens of reporters leaving the message, "We missed this time, but next time we'll get him."

After Rabin's death was announced, the same group left a follow-up message to the same reporters taking responsibility for the murder. Clearly, the person leaving the message, most likely Raviv, originally thought Amir was supposed to miss Rabin and was caught off guard when it turned out Rabin was, in fact, assassinated for real.

Maariv, November 19, 1995

As recalled, minutes after the assassination, before any reporter even knew Rabin's condition, Avishai Raviv, head of Eyal, passed on the identity of the killer. Thinking that it was a mere assassination attempt, he anonymously passed on his "We missed but we'll get him next time" message.

Dan and Eisenberg interviewing an unnamed Shabak official:

"If this wasn't a deliberate set-up," we asked, "what is? How do you react to the evidence of the bystanders who heard Raviv talk to someone on his mobile phone at the peace rally and announce that it was Amir who had shot Rabin—forty minutes before Amir's identity was released on TV and radio?"

However, the Shabak official didn't act. He said the testimony was unproven. What else could he say? If the testimony of so many people were true, then Avishai Raviv knew ahead of time that Amir was going to murder Rabin. And as an agent of the government, it was incumbent upon him to share this information with his immediate superiors in the Jewish Department of the Shabak, who in turn had to have informed their superior, the head of the Shabak, Carmi Gillon.

If Raviv had withheld his prior knowledge of Amir's intentions, then he is an accessory to murder. However, no one in the Shabak, police or government is treating him that way. He has not been charged with any crime, and was for a time hidden away in a job aiding autistic children.

Raviv's activities on the night of the assassination strongly suggest that he thought Amir was not actually going to succeed in killing Rabin. Amir was to accept responsibility for the attempted murder on behalf of Eyal and Jewish Vengeance, thereby linking the murderer to a radical, right-wing, religious organization. Thus, Raviv had no compunctions about bragging to everyone within listening distance that Amir was the shooter, forty minutes before anyone in the media knew his identity.

But Raviv, like many other Shabak agents, was duped. The supposedly benign and justifiable plan to have Amir caught in the act to promote the peace process had turned into a murder they didn't expect. Obviously caught unaware, Raviv corrected his first telephoned press announcement after Rabin's death became official.

After that, he, like many other Shabak agents, police officers, and Rabin associates, became part of a murder cover-up. They had no choice. They had all willingly conspired to keep peace alive by blaming the opposing camp for an assassination attempt. This was a crime that could end careers, smear reputations and land long prison terms. And a murderer might have no compunction about killing twice.

Chapter Three
FOUL PLAY AND DEALS

While one of Eyal's main purposes was to enroll young idealists and radicalize them, another was to eliminate political leaders. Yitzhak Rabin was not the first victim, just the most permanent. Preceding him was today's Prime Minister Binyamin Netanyahu.

One month before Rabin's assassination, on October 5, another kind of rally took place in Jerusalem. A quarter of a million people gathered to protest the government's "peace" diplomacy. The featured speaker was Binyamin Netanyahu. The sheer size of the protest, which clogged downtown Jerusalem's streets for eight blocks, shocked the promulgators of the peace process. To counterbalance the massive demonstration, two of the them, former Likud mayor of Tel Aviv, Shlomo Lahat, and a mysterious Frenchman, Jean Friedman, who had been bankrolling a campaign on behalf of the peace process, decided to organize an equally large demonstration in Tel Aviv. Even after busing in many thousands of political and youth group members (Israeli Arabs beefed up the attendance by a third), only half as many people showed up as at the protest the month before.

Just as Prime Mininster Rabin was physically assassinated at the Tel Aviv peace rally, Netanyahu withstood a character assassination at the Jerusalem rally. Avishai Raviv was once again the common denominator. Raviv displayed a posters of Rabin wearing a Gestapo uniform, a poster which Netanyahu was falsely accused of having approved. This poster led to accusations that Netanyahu created the atmosphere which led directly to Rabin's murder. Ironically, it was Rabin himself who made the accusation in the Knesset that Netanyahu was inciting violence.

The implications are profound. The Prime Minister is responsible for the Shabak and for approving its activities. Unless the Shabak dared to work behind his back, Rabin approved the Raviv operation, thus signing his own death warrant.

> *Yediot Ahronot,* November 19, 1995
> According to testimony from Judea and Samaria Council spokesman Aharon Domev; Avishai Raviv along with other

Eyal people were seen on the night of the demonstration in Zion Square (Jerusalem), October 5, distributing the poster.

Yediot Ahronot, November 20, 1995
Channel One reporter, Nitzan Khen, told viewers of last night's news program that just a few minutes before beginning to broadcast from the demonstration of the right at Zion Square, he was given a leaflet showing Rabin in a Gestapo uniform by Avishai Raviv.
Khen: "Raviv came up to me with two other people known to me, an Eyal activist and Kach member. They came to the broadcast van and gave me the leaflet. After five or ten minutes Raviv returned to make sure I had broadcast it."

Yediot Ahronot, December 11, 1995
Police Captain Yehuda Saidoff: "I concluded that Nitzan Khen has a wild imagination and poor memory for facts. Raviv was more believable to me." Raviv told Saidoff that he received just one copy of the leaflet from a yeshivah student named Aharon Victor and when he got home, he ripped it up.

Yediot Ahronot, November 27, 1995
In Jerusalem yesterday, a 16-year-old yeshivah student was remanded for three days for distributing a leaflet of Yitzhak Rabin in an SS uniform at the rally in Zion Square. He admitted guilt and was said he regretted his actions. According to him, Avishai Raviv was responsible for distributing the leaflet.

Maariv, November 27, 1995
The police will question Avishai Raviv on suspicion that he distributed leaflets showing Rabin in an SS uniform at the right-wing rally at Zion Square. One of the two arrested Yeshivah students had close ties to Raviv. Police will question other yeshivah students to establish the extent of the suspect's ties with Raviv.

At the time of the demonstration, when Rabin was very much alive, the issue of who distributed the leaflet was marginal. It didn't

matter who distributed it, the issue was that Netanyahu didn't condemn the blown-up poster and leaflets from the podium. It was a
phony issue, Netanyahu couldn't and didn't see the posters from the
stage. But when he tried to explain that fact to the Knesset, Rabin
indignantly walked out of the chamber.

At the time, it seemed Rabin had every right to put on his show
of anger. But within two weeks of his death, the public knew about
Raviv's role in the Shabak and the issue looked quite different.
Nitzan Khen testified at the Shamgar Commission hearings that
Raviv and another Eyal member gave him the leaflet of Rabin in a
Gestapo uniform. As Defense Minister Rabin was responsible for
Shabak activities, he should have known exactly who Raviv and Eyal
were. At the most, he approved the poster operation. At the least, he
knew it was a Shabak ploy to weaken opposition to the peace pro-
cess. Either way, by walking out of the Knesset while Netanyahu was
speaking, he was toying with his political rival.

Rabin was certainly motivated. At that point, Netanyahu was
leading Rabin in the polls by over 18% and a crowd exceeding
200,000 in a city of fewer than 400,000 Jews had gathered to support him.

The country was not divided in two over peace. The vast major-
ity had soured on the process. The month before, a *Maariv* poll
revealed that 78% of Israelis wanted a national referendum on
whether to carry on the government's peace diplomacy. Members of
the government were booed whenever they appeared in public, but
none more so than Rabin. In August, 50,000 fans at a soccer game
between Israel and Brazil jeered in unison when he arrived. Not
long after, he was humiliated when his speech before one thousand
English speaking immigrants was marred by the loudest uniformly
loud long boo ever heard in Netanya.

A constant vigil of protesters stood outside Rabin's home in sub-
urban Tel Aviv. But, none was so vicious as the Eyal crowd who
promised that he and his wife would hang in a public square like the
Mussolinis, thus beginning the sophisticated game of delegitimizing
legal protest through extra-legal extremism. Raviv and his cohorts
could only have gotten away with it with the cooperation of the
police, and Police Minister Moshe Shahal; the same Shahal who was
sending mounted policemen into crowds to club thousands of anti-

government demonstrators. Indeed, Raviv was held for questioning by the police for the Rabin poster, but as in every previous case where the police questioned him, he was released shortly after. The public trusted Nitzan Khen, the Channel One reporter, and believed him when he testified to the Shamgar Commission that Avishai Raviv gave him the infamous leaflet. And yet, Captain Saidoff took the side of the notorious extremist, Raviv, over that of the respected journalist, Khen. Such an inexplicable conclusion only demonstrates the wide-ranging pattern of a cover-up of Eyal's activities by the police and Justice Ministry.

> Marc Weiss writes in *The Jewish Press,* April 25, 1997:
> Apparently, the Israeli Justice Department had been informed of Raviv's true identity and informant status, and was instructed not to bring agent "Champagne" to trial for his illegal actions. In a document obtained by the *Jewish Press,* the Special Branch of the Israeli Police that deals with extremist groups wrote to Raviv on February 21, 1994 informing him that they were closing their files and declining to prosecute him for the charges of "incitement" against the government. Ironically, the document cites "the lack of public interest" in Raviv's provocations as the reason.

This document, which revealed Raviv's repeated declarations about the dire need and biblical permissibility of killing Rabin (incitements that laid the very foundation for Yigal Amir's actions), is startling in its implications. Time and again, Raviv was permitted by the State Prosecutor's office to continue on with his campaign of provocation without fear of arrest or prison. Why was Raviv never seriously prosecuted and why didn't Attorney General Michael Ben-Yair order the Shabak to immediately curtail its illegal undercover activities?

> *Yediot Ahronot,* November 24, 1995
> I can't believe the government itself distributed the leaflet showing the Prime Minister in a Nazi uniform. I'm certain the Shabak would never have gone ahead with this kind of operation on its own. However, the government exploited the issue

viciously to wound the rival political camp which is made up of half the population.

Maariv, November 20, 1995
The editorial staff of Maariv asks the police and Justice Ministry—Why haven't you revealed which printing house published the leaflet and why haven't you found the person who ordered the printing?

Yediot Ahronot, November 20, 1995
Since Rabin's murder, claim Likud spokespeople, their political opposition has waged a cynical campaign aimed at blaming them for the incitement culminating with the poster of Rabin in a Nazi uniform, which led to the murder.

Benjamin Begin*: "Did the Shabak report to the politicians, before or after the rally, that their agent Raviv distributed the leaflets of the Prime Minister in a Nazi uniform?"

The difficult question is, did the political establishment know of Raviv's responsibility and cynically exploit it to gain politically by humiliating Binyamin Netanyahu?

Says Binyamin Netanyahu: "If even a part of what is being revealed is true, then there exists a serious threat to our democracy. We demand a full inquiry. We won't permit a cover-up."

Immediately after the assassination, the media broadcast numerous claims that Netanyahu killed Rabin by creating the atmosphere which bred the killer. The proof of this absurd contention, was always the poster of Rabin in the SS garb which he allegedly refused to condemn.

The Justice Ministry, aided by police, exploited this pre-assassination incitement, to initiate a campaign of repression. The Justice Ministry passed a law making a broad definition of incitement illegal. The roundups began.

Three rabbis accused of declaring Rabin a persecutor were held for questioning and one was imprisoned without charge for months.

---

* Son of Kikud founder Menachem Begin. He was originally Netanyahu's Science Minister, but quit over the Hebron withdrawal.

An Israeli farmer who expressed satisfaction with the murder during a CNN interview was imprisoned for expressing an inciteful point of view. Shmuel Cytryn of Hebron, who exposed Raviv as a Shabak agent two months before the assassination, was arrested and imprisoned in solitary confinement for four months without ever being charged. Dozens of political opponents were arrested and jailed under Administrative Detention orders which permit arrest without charge. A well prepared clampdown and witchhunt of people opposed to the peace process gripped the nation. Within eight hours of the murder, hundreds of billboards appeared throughout the country reading, "Rabin Is Making Peace in Heaven." How the graphics, printing, and construction of these signs were accomplished so quickly has never been investigated.

Netanyahu was humiliated time and again for his alleged role in the poster scandal. While Leah Rabin greeted Yasir Arafat in her home during the grieving period, she refused to host Netanyahu or even shake his hand when he offered condolences again at the funeral. A year later when he was Prime Minister, his attendance at a memorial service for Rabin was marred by protesters accusing him of creating the atmosphere of hatred that spawned the murder.

But by then he was well aware of the truth. During his election campaign, he had promised if elected to prosecute the Shabak provocateur, Avishai Raviv.

Yet after the assassination, while he was being vilified, he failed to demand a commission of inquiry into Raviv's activities. After his election, he broke his promise to prosecute Raviv.

Why wouldn't he want his good name and the good name of his party cleared?

Natan Gefen, a diligent researcher of the assassination, best known for acquiring the controversial and contentious death certificate from Ichilov Hospital certifying that Rabin was shot by an extra bullet in his chest, thinks he knows why.

"Before the election, I took the [death] certificate to two Likud Knesset Members, Yossi Olmert and Dov Shilansky, fully expecting them to consider the political advantages of it. Olmert told me the Likud wouldn't touch the Rabin issue. They didn't need to.

"A deal was cut, I'm sure of it. Labor didn't bring up Rabin's memory during the campaign and neither did the Likud. Peres

[Netanyahu's opponent] stopped campaigning altogether; he threw the television debate with Netanyahu, he was leading in all the polls by 4% the morning of the vote and he still lost. Netanyahu got the full story from sympathizers in the Shabak and he agreed to hush it up in return for winning power. That's why the cover-up is still going on like nothing changed after the elections."

Gefen's intuition proved right. Two months later I was invited to a Cabinet Minister's office. The Minister's chief aide informed me that the Likud had prepared a file that contained specific information about Rabin's murder that would be released publicly if the Labor party utilized Rabin's name in the election campaign, or if Peres won the election.

Chapter Four
TELEVISION SETS UP AMIR

One of Raviv's assignments was to create the most radical anti-peace group and to publicize it widely. Eyal's original purpose to attract extremists and set them up for arrest was later expanded to cultivate Amir, as an assassin. Eyal's well-known reputation for extremism was essential to the plot. Amir's mere association with it would be seen as motive enough for murder.

To achieve this goal, Raviv needed help from the television medium. He got it in the form of Eitan Oren, a documentary director employed by the state-run television station, Channel One.

Moti Kirschenbaum was appointed as Director General of Channel One in 1992 by Rabin himself. Two years later the station was bankrupt. He had eliminated fourteen hours of entertainment programing and replaced them with political shows that heavily promoted the peace process. Kirschenbaum's allegiances were obvious. One time, Channel One news covered an anti-Rabin rally, much to the Prime Minister's displeasure. It was widely reported that Rabin's wife, Leah, phoned Kirschenbaum and related, how upset Yitzhak is that the protesters received so much coverage."Kirschenbaum immediately initiated a unofficial policy change drastically reducing coverage time of legitimate protests.

Channel One's news department sent Oren time and again to cover Eyal's illegimate protests. Two young Eyal members, Erin Agelbo and Arieh Oranj, recount their "protest" experiences as stage directed by both Oren and Raviv with Raviv actually paying their expenses. Not the hotheaded extremists one would expect, these two kids remain terrified of Shabak threats to prosecute them if they were to come forward with further information on Raviv and Amir.

To further understand how Channel One and Oren were used to prepare the public for Rabin's assassination, I turn to reports from the Israeli press, collected by Miriam Eilon in one volume called "The Champagne File."

Maariv, November 24, 1995
A young Haredi, no more than eighteen, explained, "I'm a yeshiva student and don't have money. Raviv paid all my travel and food expenses. He also promised me more money each time I got Eyal's name mentioned in the media."

Hatsofeh, February 17, 1995
Over 500 people attended a memorial service in honor of Baruch Goldstein ... Among the organizers was Avishai Raviv, head of Eyal. Many members of the media were also in attendance.

Hatsofeh, February 17, 1995
Head of Eyal, Avishai Raviv, promised to get even with members of the Judea and Samaria Council who condemned his organization of the Baruch Goldstein memorial service, including Council Secretary Uri Ariel and Council spokesman Aharon Domev. According to Raviv, "The loss of Goldstein wasn't equal to all the Arabs he killed."

Maariv, February 17, 1995
Head of the Kiryat Arba city council, Tzi Katzover is threatening to file suit with the Supreme Court to prevent the showing of a television report about Kiryat Arba. In a letter he sent to Communications Minister Shulamit, Aloni Katzover contends that the reporter, Eitan Oren staged scenes opposite a

poster honoring Baruch Goldstein. "We don't know what else
he staged for his upcoming report," said Katzover.

Months before Rabin's death, Avishai Raviv organized, and Eitan
Oren covered, a memorial service in honor of mass murderer
Baruch Goldstein.* Oren and Raviv orchestrated at least one extra-
radical scene.
Raviv dressed up twenty teenagers in t-shirts bearing the name of
the right-wing Kach movement, and Oren filmed them in the midst
of mock guerilla warfare.

> *Haaretz,* August 5, 1994
> Last Friday night Channel One broadcast a report about a
> Kach teenage militia training camp whose existence is illegal.
> Kach symbols and flags were filmed as well as youths wearing
> Kach t-shirts. Shown also was a patrol in an Arab village and
> the youths writing inciteful grafitti.

The Oren news program was broadcast on a Friday night, several days after the incident, when the most religious Jews are forbidden to watch television. The less devout population was repulsed by
the display of an irrational Jewish Nationalism, though the event
was actually condemned by the Jewish territorial leadership.

> In light of the report, Police Minister Moshe Shahal has
> ordered an immediate investigation. The police searched for
> Avishai Raviv but he disappeared. He later phoned the police
> and agreed to show up on Sunday for questioning. Yesterday,
> he told *Haaretz*, "We organized the camp to show our solidar-
> ity with the people of Hebron and Kiryat Arba. We trained in
> live weaponry, orienteering, took a hike to Baruch Goldstein's
> grave and participated in other youth group activities."

Raviv admitted that he and his friends initiated the media expo-
sure in order to raise public awareness.

---

* The circumstances of the Hebron massacre and Goldstein's role parallel
  the Rabin assassination in too many ways and are fit subject for a separate book.

Maariv, November 24, 1995
"We immediately knew that Raviv never studied at a yeshiva associated with Kach," said Kach leader Baruch Marzel. "His behaviour towards Jews and Arabs was inconsistent with our approach. We would never call another Jew a Nazi. He came to us and asked us to join in a national union of right-wing groups. We turned him down. We would never cause the kind of damage to the community that he did."

Maariv, November 24, 1995
Kach member Tsuriel Popovich witnessed Raviv in action. "I saw him beat an old Arab senseless for no reason. If an Arab looked at him or his group, he risked his life. Raviv was causing a lot of trouble for us because we all suffered the stigma he was creating."

Kach's spiritual leader Rabbi Meir Kahane was assassinated five years to the week before the assassination of Rabin. His death was mired in equally suspicious circumstances. But while Rabin was portrayed as a saint after his demise by the Israeli media, Kahane continued to be vilified. Thus Raviv, by dressing his actors in Kach costumes, tapped into a most invidious existing public image.

On September 22, a month and a half before Rabin's demise, Channel One broadcast Oren's report of an Eyal swearing-in ceremony at the grave of Zionism's founder, Theodore Herzl.

Erin Agelbo recalls, "Raviv's little play was so ridiculous we spent much of the time laughing. Oren filmed us for over 45 minutes and edited it down to 10 minutes for television. My lawyer tried to get the uncut tape from Channel One but no one would hand it over and the police refused to confiscate it."

Maariv, November 24, 1995
An 18-year-old haredi boy who participated in the swearing-in ceremony recalls, "None of the participants were Eyal members because Eyal didn't exist except for Raviv and Agelbo."

In Eitan Oren's report, a hooded boy holding a gun vows to kill anybody, Jew or Arab, who stands in the way of Eyal's objectives. "I arrived at seven in the evening," says the haredi boy, "and saw Raviv distributing ski masks to the others. He told us what to do, what to say, where to stand. Agelbo told me, 'You have a nice voice, you swear everyone in.'

"I don't know what Eitan Oren thought but he knew the whole thing was staged. There was one scene where Raviv demonstrated how he beat new members to make them confess if they were with the Shabak. It looked so absurd that we all burst-out laughing. It's no shock that Eitan Oren didn't keep that scene in his film."

Yediot Ahronot, November 26, 1995
Police arrested Erin Agelbo and Mosh Erinfeld for their participation in an Eyal swearing-in ceremony filmed by Eitan Oren and broadcast on Channel One on September 22. In the ceremony, new members vowed to "spill the blood of Arabs and Jews who aren't Jews," as well as to break into Orient House in Jerusalem.

Maariv, November 24, 1995
During a previous swearing-in ceremony, Avishai Raviv left two minutes before two squad cars of police arrived to arrest the participants.

Only the active participation and influence of Kirschenbaum and Oren can explain Eyal's disproportionate television covverage.

An associate of Oren's, who wishes to remain anonymous, said, "He is such an idealogue that he got ethically unbalanced, believing he was doing the wrong thing for the right cause." Perhaps, but someone at Channel One assigned Oren to Eyal, and Moti Kirschenbaum approved the broadcasts.

A few weeks before the assassination…

Yediot Ahronot, November 20, 1995
A patrol through Hebron which included Yigal Amir made the news. The group first broke windows of Arab houses and then smashed the camera of a Palestinian news photographer.

After this incident and just two weeks before the assassination, Yigal Amir was filmed being taken away by the police kicking and screaming during an anti-government demonstration in Efrat. That clip was shown on Channel One just hours after Rabin was murdered. And the next day on Channel One, numerous commentators blamed the "anti-peace" community, a community of more than half the country, for Rabin's death.

The public immediately accepted Amir's guilt because he was a member of the extremist Eyal group. The Shabak's covert umbilical to Eyal remained hidden.

Chapter Five
HOW DID THE SHABAK MISS AMIR AT THE RALLY?

It is the solemn duty of any head of state's security detail to research and prepare for all contingencies. They must identify particularly threatening individuals and most especially be trained to identify (and eliminate) even a threatening gesture.

Not only was Amit's affiliation to Eyal known to the Shabak and literally hundreds of Bar Ilan Iniversity students, apparently he was familiar to the filmmaker of the assassination who focused on him for a suspiciously long time.

Take the famous case of Shlomi Halevy, a reserve soldier in the IDF's Intelligence Brigade and a fellow student of Amir's at Bar Ilan University. After being informed that Amir was talking about killing Rabin, he reported the information to his superior officer in the brigade. He told Halevy to go to the police immediately. Halevy told them "a short Yemenite in Eyal was boasting that he was going to assassinate Rabin." The police took Halevy very seriously and transferred his report to the Shabak—where it sat for four months and wasn't "discovered" until three days after Rabin's assassination.

The weekly news magazine *Yerushalayim* on September 22, 1996 managed to convince Halevy to give his first interview since the discovery of his report and the subsequent media fallout. The magazine noted, "Halevy's and other reports of Amir's intentions which

gathered dust in Shabak files have fueled numerous conspiracy theories. After the uproar, Halevy went into hiding."

"Shlomi Levy, if you did the right thing why have you hidden
from the public?"

"The assassination is a sore point with the Shabak. They're big
and I'm little. I didn't know what they could do to me."

Halevy was the most publicized case since as a soldier in the
Intelligence Brigade, the Shabak was required to take his evidence as
seriously as did the police. But Halevy was not the only one to step
forward.

> *Yediot Ahronot,* November 12, 1995
> A number of weeks before the Rabin assassination, the Shabak
> received information about the existence of Yigal Amir and
> his intention to murder Yitzhak Rabin.
>
> *Yediot Ahronot* was informed that one of the Eyal activists
> arrested last week was interrogated for being a possible co-con-
> spirator of Yigal Amir's. The assassin's brother Haggai had
> mentioned him in his own interrogation.
>
> At the beginning of his interrogation, the suspect broke
> down into bitter tears, telling a tale that was initially viewed as
> ridiculous by his interrogators. Weeks before the murder, the
> suspect had heard Amir speak his intentions and he was
> shocked. He was torn between informing the authorities and
> betraying his fellows, so he chose a middle route. He would
> give away Amir's intentions without naming him.
>
> After some hesitation, he informed a police intelligence
> officer about Amir's plan in detail, stopping just short of iden-
> tifying him or his address. He told them where Amir studied
> and described him as a "short, dark Yemenite with curly hair."
>
> The description was passed along the police communica-
> tions network and classified as important. The information
> was also passed to the Shabak, officers of which subsequent-
> ly took a statement from the suspect. Because he was in a
> delicate position, neither the police or Shabak pressed him
> further.
>
> While being interrogated, the suspect named the police
> and Shabak officers involved and his story was confirmed. He

was then released. Shabak officials confirmed that the man had previously given them a description of Amir and his plan to murder Rabin.

Maariv, November 19, 1995
Hila Frank knew Amir well from her studies at Bar Ilan. After the assassination, she hired a lawyer and told him that she had heard, well before the event, Amir state his intention to murder Rabin. As a member of the campus Security Committee, she organized anti-government demonstrations. Thus, she was torn between exposing Amir's intentions and the interests of the state.

To overcome the dilemma, she passed on her information to Shlomi Halevy, a reserve soldier in the Intelligence Brigade who promised that it would be given to the right people.

Yerushalayim, November 17, 1995
Why wasn't a drawing of Amir based on Halevy's description distributed to the Prime Minister's security staff? Why didn't they interrogate other Eyal activists to discover who the man threatening to kill the Prime Minister was?

Yediot Ahronot, November 10, 1995
A month and a half before the assassination, journalist Yaron Kenner pretended to be a sympathizer and spent two days at a study sabbath in Hebron organized by Yigal Amir.

"Who organized this event?" I asked. He pointed to Yigal Amir. He had invited 400 and over 540 arrived. This caused organizational havoc.

When Amir spoke, people quieted down, testifying to some charisma. On the other hand, his soft tone and unimpressive stature wouldn't have convinced anyone to buy even a popsicle from him.

Maariv, December 12, 1995
During his "Identity Weekends," hundreds of people heard Amir express his radical thoughts, amongst which were his biblical justifications for the murder of Rabin.

Yediot Ahronot, November 24, 1995
Yigal Amir turned into an object of attention for the Shabak
beginning six months ago when he started organizing study
weekends in Kiryat Arba and they requested a report on him.
Raviv prepared the report.

Maariv, November 24, 1995
A carful of Bar Ilan students were driving from Tel Aviv when
they heard the announcement of Rabin's shooting on the
radio. They played a game, each thinking of five people who
might have done it. Yigal Amir was on all their lists.

Yigal Amir did not keep his intentions to assassinate Rabin a
secret. He told many hundreds of people gathered at his study weekends and seems to have told everyone within hearing distance at Bar
Ilan University. And still, on the night of April 11, 1995, he was
allowed free access to the Prime Minister.

Clearly wittingly or not, Yigal Amir was working for the Shabak.

Chapter Six
DRY RUN

In early September 1994 the Shabak and police proclaimed that
they had busted the Vengeance Underground, a Jewish militia that
planned to stage terrorist attacks against Arab villages and the center of PLO activities in Jerusalem, Orient House. Seventeen Jews
were arrested and held without charge for days in inhuman condi-
tions. (One incarcerated man's severely rat-bitten face led to a
national scandal.) Eventually, the seventeen were charged with conspiracy to commit murder. Only two of the accused, however, actually knew each other, two brothers, Yehoyada and Eitan Kahalani.
Eventually charges were dropped against all except the Kahalani
brothers.

Their story began with a bit of over-opportunistic capitalism.
State-controlled marketing of produce in Israel results in food prod-
ucts, including eggs, being very overpriced. The Kahalanis planned

to go into business smuggling eggs with Kiryat Arba neighbor, Yves Tibi. The three were to buy eggs from a West Bank Arab producer at a fraction of the cost of Israeli eggs, and sell them in Israel proper.

On September 2, 1994, the brothers went scouting routes out of the West Bank, driving through obscure villages. On their way back to Kiryat Arba, their truck inexplicably broke down and could not climb the hill into Jerusalem. They called Tibi, explained their dilemma and asked to borrow his car. He agreed and everyone met in Jerusalem at 2 PM. The Kahalanis brothers drove away in Tibi's car and at 2:13 passed through Batir, an Arab village within Jerusalem. Literally two minutes later a Shabak jeep waiting in ambush stopped them. They were forced out of the car at gunpoint and the car was searched. Two M-16 automatic rifles were found tightly wrapped in a blanket. A police squad car arrived shortly after and the brothers were arrested. They were held in a Shabak lockup without being charged and unable to see a lawyer for a week and a half. Ten days later, on September 12, they were charged with attempted murder when an Arab named Ziad Shami stepped forward to file a complaint that while riding his bicycle to work in Batir, the brothers had attempted to shoot him, but the rifle misfired. Three days later, the Shabak explained that it had rigged the brothers' rifles to prevent them from shooting in order to catch them red-handed. In fact, I was given a weapons check report from the Police Ballstics lab, signed by Shechter,[*] proving the rifles were in police custody the day before the alleged shooting.

Ziad Shami's connection to this case was questionable from the first. He had, on several occasions been arrested by the Shabak for violent activities and was actually imprisoned twice. His accounts of the attack were numerous and contradictory. During one police interview he claimed to have heard the rifle tick and seen a cartridge fall. Later he said he heard nothing and only saw one brother fire bending from behind the car. During one interview he said he could identify his assailants, then later recanted. During the trial, an employee of Shami's was brought in to substantiate his testimony. He testified that Shami had told him about the incident two days after it happened. But, under cross-examination, he was confronted with a time card that showed that Shami had been to work the day

---

[*] Shechter is the same officer who examined Amir's weapons.

immediately following the shooting. Why didn't he tell him then?
He then decided he had actually told him the previous day.

Shami's testimony was consistent only in that it consistently
evolved to fit the charges: he left his bicycle, he took it; he saw, he
didn't see; he heard, he didn't hear; a friend picked him up on the
road, a stranger picked him up; he was confronted at point blank
range, then it was back several paces. He even told the police that
the brothers' first words to him were, "What's the time?" Then in
court he testified that they had first asked, "Do you have any
money?"

There were forensic inconsistencies as well. At first it was released
that the rifles were wiped clean of fingerprints. Later it was discov-
ers that there were fingerprints on the weapons, but none matched
the brothers'. The police tested all seventeen suspects' prints and yet
none matched those on the weapon. Yves Tibi was, inexplicably,
never tested. Also Police Warrant Officer Zeiger testified that a bullet clip was pulled out of the brothers' backpack at the time of arrest.
Their fingerprints weren't on it. Further, the police log of September
2, 1994 reports that the clip was found in the defendants' home.

Despite the overwhelmingly convoluted prosecution of the
Kahalani brothers, the court found them guilty of attempted
murder.

"That verdict," says one well-placed source, "was directly related
to the assassination. If the Kahalani brothers' sting operation did
not result in a conviction, people might have started asking questions about Yigal Amir. I asked associates in the Shabak how the
brothers could have been convicted in the face of such an abundance of obviously doctored evidence. They told me there was just
one possible answer: 'At the highest levels of the Shabak, there was
a policy to discredit the settlers in order to justify their forced
removal at some stage of the peace process.'"

With this strategy in mind, Rabin was supposedly assassinated by
a right-wing Sephardic Jew who sympathized with the settler movement. The day after the assassination, the roundup of hundreds of
Jewish opponents of "peace" began and few complained. Within
weeks, the Israeli army pulled out of six West Bank regions.

In February 1996, the Kahalani brothers were to appear for sen-
tencing. Only Eitan arrived to hear his 12 year sentence. A few

weeks earlier, Yehodaya was transferred to another cellblock. He was speaking to his mother on the phone when an other inmate attacked him with an iron pipe. His last words to his mother were, "They put me in here with murderers." He survived the incident.

Chapter Seven
FROM THE MOUTHS OF THE SHABAK

Following Rabin's assassination, the head of the Shabak, Carmi Gillon, his two officers in charge of Jewish radicals and their agent Avishai Raviv, found themselves mired in controversy. Someone had revealed the truth about Raviv.

Gillon's first step was to appoint his own internal commission of inquiry, but the public was not satisfied. The government then appointed its own commission of inquiry headed by the former Chief Justice of the Israeli Supreme Court, Meir Shamgar. He sent letters to seven Shabak officers including Gillon and Jewish Activities Department head Kheshin, and yet overlooked his own colleague, Eli Barak, who oversaw the Raviv operation. In these letters, Shamgar informed each that he was liable for criminal prosecution. Some of their testimony was made public, though approximately 30 percent remains undisclosed due to concerns for state security. Because most of the Shabak principals' testimony to the Shamgar Commission was withheld from the public, one must look to whatever sources are available. As paltry as they are, they are revealing.

Carmi Gillon, from his 1990 Master's Thesis:

> Israeli society displays tolerance toward ideological lawbreakers of the extreme right and this grants, albeit belatedly, legitimacy to these activities.

Yediot Ahronot, November 10, 1995
A group of journalists met Carmi Gillon at the end of August. Among other things, he painted a portrait of a potential Jewish assassin of the Prime Minister. Without knowing it, he described Yigal Amir perfectly. He would be someone who

didn't live in the territories, said the Shabak head. He will be
not be a joiner but an almost wise loner.

Gillon's Master's Thesis:

> The process of extremism in Israeli society is creating individ-
> uals who will ignore danger in pursuit of their goals.

> *Yediot Ahronot,* November 20, 1995
> Quotes from the head of the Shabak at the Shamgar
> Commission are teaching us his defense. He is calling Amir a
> "lone nut" who awoke one day and decided to murder the
> Prime Minister without anyone's help. He claims nuts like
> these are very hard to identify so the murder was not caused
> by an "intelligence breakdown."

This is a very problematic defence. Although Amir has testified
that he worked alone, other evidence suggests that three or four
other people were in on the secret. Amir was not exactly anti-social.
Gillon's "lone nut" theory is groundless.

> *Yediot Ahronot,* November 24, 1995
> The head of the Shabak had no doubt who the assassin was.
> The moment he was informed of the close-range shooting by
> long distance phone, his first reaction was, "It was a Jew."

Avraham Rotem, former head of Personal Security for the
Shabak, in *Maariv* in November 1995, expressed great reservation
about Gillon's non-role in the assassination.

> "Where was the head of the Shabak last Saturday night?
> Abroad. What was he doing there? Not known. Something
> urgent. What's more urgent than protecting the life of the
> Prime Minister? He didn't know someone was going to
> murder Rabin.
> He didn't know? So why is it written in the papers that a
> few months ago he warned Rabin that someone from the
> extreme right is planning to assassinate him? And then he

went to the heads of the political parties to give the same
warning and request that they prevent incitement to murder?
You can't tell the Prime Minister that someone is going to
murder him and then go back to routine security procedures.

Was it a coincidence that Gillon warned politicians, journalists
and even Rabin himself of an impending assassination attempted by
an almost-wise loner who didn't live in the territories? He persis-
tently defended himself by calling Amir a "lone nut," denying any
possible Shabak involvment.

And yet, forty-eight hours before the assassination, Gillon flew to
Paris for unknown urgent business despite pleas from subordinates
not to leave before the rally.

Shamgar let Gillon off with a wrist slap.

Officer Kheshin is the most mysterious Shabak figure surrounding the assassination, his first name isn't even known. Eli Barak—
head of the Jewish Department of the Shabak, is known to have
been Raviv's superior, but no one has properly defined Kheshin's
role. All we know is that he was Barak's immediate superior.

Maariv reported on December 18, 1995, that the Shamgar
Commission was examining the contradictions between police testimony and that of Officer Kheshin—"They are asking how the
Shabak reacted to information coming out of Bar Ilan University
and why the Shabak was ignorant of the Shabbat activities in Judea
and Samaria organized by Yigal Amir with Avishai Raviv."

> *Yediot Ahronot,* November 22, 1995
> According to the head of the Department of Jewish Activities
> [Kheshin] during six hours of testimony at the Shamgar
> Commission, the Shabak requested that Raviv supply them
> with an overview of Amir's activities three months before the
> assassination.
>
> Raviv returned from his field duties and told them of
> Amir's intention to harm Arabs. Kheshin testified, "Raviv
> didn't know Amir's real intentions and did not inform us of
> his plans to harm Jews, including the Prime Minister."

Maariv, December 19, 1995

Among those most surprised by the warning letter from Shamgar was Kheshin, who believes the cause of Rabin's assassination was a security, not intelligence breakdown. He believes the warning to him was totally unjustified.

Kheshin, the head of the Jewish Activities Department, claimed he knew nothing of Yigal Amir's threats to Rabin at Bar Ilan University. Furthermore, he said he had received a report from agent Avishai Raviv three months prior to the murder that made no mention of the threats Raviv must have heard on numerous occasions.

Kheshin insisted he was told instead that Amir wanted to beat up Arabs. And yet, the frail Amir refused to participate in any of Raviv's many Arab-beating raids into Hebron, until the fateful occassion, he was fortuitously filmed in action shortly before the assassination.

If it's true, Raviv deliberately hid the truth about Amir from Kheshin just as his other subordinates kept the intelligence from Bar Ilan University from him.

~

Eli Barak headed The Non-Arab Anti-Subversive Unit of the Shabak, a commonly known as the Jewish Department. Kheshin was known to be his superior officer, suggesting that the Jewish Activities Department and the Jewish Department are separate entities. However, since 30 percent of the Shamgar Commission report which remains classified includes information on the Shabak's departmental infrastructure, the exact nature of the chain of command is not known. And because Shamgar excluded Barak from testifying in open session, only some testimony has surfaced.

Yediot Ahronot, November 20, 1995

According to the London newspaper, *The Observor,* high Israeli security officials claim that officers of the Shabak knew Yigal Amir's intention to murder Yitzhak Rabin. The highest ranking officer who knew was Eli Barak, head of the Jewish Department, who didn't take Amir's "ridiculous plans" seriously. The newspaper doesn't explain why Barak didn't pass on

Amir's threats to the head of the Shabak and that the answer to this will have to come out at the commission of inquiry.

Maariv, November 27, 1995
Eli Barak, head of the department which deals with Jewish extremists, testified that Avishai Raviv didn't know that Yigal Amir intended to murder Yitzhak Rabin. He only reported that Amir was an activist at Bar Ilan University. According to Barak, Amir decided on his own to murder Rabin and no one could have stopped him.

The former head of the Mossad, Committee member Tzvi Zamir, asked Barak to explain why the Shabak didn't act on Shlomi Halevy's report to the police that a short, Yemenite member of Eyal was threatening Rabin. The committee stressed that because Halevi was a soldier of the Intelligence Brigade, serious attention should have been given to his claims.

Barak's answer was never published. But, it is known that while Kheshin claimed to have been ignorant of Amir's campus radicalism, Raviv chose to inform Barak about it. However, both agree that agent Raviv didn't know Amir had any plans to murder Rabin.

∽

We know that Avishai Raviv must have been a Shabak agent since 1987. At that time the deacon of Tel Aviv University, Elyakim Rubinstein, tried to expel him for extremist activities. Then Prime Minister Shamir sent his aide Yossi Achimeir to intervene with Rubinstein on Raviv's behalf.

Finding quotes from Raviv that aren't saturated with staged extremism is difficult. But, in November 1996, the news magazine *Kol Ha'ir* confronted him and he admitted, "No one would believe what I know and can't tell."

It is now known that Raviv lied at the trial of Haggai Amir, when he told the court, "I never worked for or was associated with the Shabak." And the fact that his testimony went without protest is evidence itself of a great miscarriage of justice.

In January 1998, Hagai Amir finally sued Raviv. He charged that had Raviv not perjured himself, his sentence would have been much lighter. In March, the Shabak put his brother, Yigal, in his cell with him for two days until Hagai decided to drop his suit. One can only guess why Yigal Amir was so interested in protecting Avishai Raviv.

Chapter Eight
THE CONTIGENCY THAT WASN'T USED

The Shabak claimed they were unprepared for a lone gunman on that fateful night at King's of Israel Square.

And yet, two former officers of the Shabak's personal security unit claim that when they were in command, they had prepared detailed contingency plans, in the early 1990's, against a lone assassin—including one for King of Israel Square. As reported in *Anashim* magazine, it even included an assassin standing at the exit stairs behind the stage, precisely as Yigal Amir had. The officers, Tuvia Livneh and Yisrael Shai, interviewed in the same article, expressed bewilderment and frustration. Livneh, "When Yisrael and I heard the news of the murder we became infuriated at the fact that there was a contingency plan for just such an attempt, which we practiced endless times."

What further baffled Livneh and Shai was the fact that security personnels' primary directive after failing to secure the field, was to first shield the Prime Minister and secondly eliminate the assassin. When the Anashim reporter asked, "For years you trained your people to kill the assassin, but when the real thing happened, they didn't do a thing." Livneh replied, "I suppose that when an unknown man shouted, 'they're blanks,' he stopped the guards in their tracks."

Livneh continues, "I stress that I have no personal information, but it's reasonable to assume that one of Amir's co-conspirators, whether known or unknown, stood near him in the crowd and aided him in this way. Or maybe it was Amir, after all."

Shortly after Amir was arrested, a police interrogator asked him, "Did you shout that the bullets were blanks?"

"Why would I do that?" Amir replied.

"To throw the bodyguards off your trail. To temporarily confuse them."

"An interesting idea," Amir replied, "But I didn't do it."

In fact, "Srak, srak," meaning, "They're blanks, blanks," was far from the only thing shouted after the shooting. Bodyguards yelled a variety of similar sentences including,

"It was nothing." "It's an exercise." "It's not real." "Caps." "Toy gun," etc.

Since Amir could not have shouted from eight or nine different locations, it wasn't him. If there were other conspirators, they would have had to have been bodyguards.

The article continues:

> Livneh and Shai were pleased when the Shamgar Commission was formed and waited patiently to be called to testify. Both were considered the leading experts on personal security in the country. Both served for years in the unit and were the personal bodyguards of such central figures as Golda Meir, Moshe Dayan, Ezer Weizmann and of Rabin himself during his first term in office; both knew the service inside out and rose through the ranks until they became its commanders, first Livneh, then Shai.

But the Shamgar Commission ignored them.

Livneh concludes, "There was nothing new about the murder, nothing we hadn't taken into account in the past. The fact that the murderer was able to complete his mission was the humiliating fault of those responsible for personal security that night."

Not one Shabak officer responsible for Rabin's security was tried, court martialed, or imprisoned. The worst punishment meted out was forced resignation.

Chapter Nine
THE KEMPLER FILM

Almost two months after the Rabin assassination, Israelis were shocked to read in their newspapers that an amateur had filmed the event and it would be shown on Channel Two news. The filmmaker was at first announced as a Polish tourist. However, this story changed the day of the broadcast. The filmmaker was, in fact, an Israeli named Roni Kempler. Kempler was no ordinary citizen. He worked for the State Comptroller's Office and was a bodyguard in the army reserves.

It is an extremely rare occurrence when the Israeli press publishes an opinion that expresses doubt about the veracity of the Shamgar Commission. Yet in the aftermath of an expose written in *Maariv* on September 27, 1996 on the testimony of GSS (Shabak) agents and police officers present near the murder site, several responses were published. One was from Labour Knesset Member Ofir Pines, who admitted he too heard numerous security agents shout that the shots which supposedly felled Rabin were blanks. He added rather weakly that, in retrospect, perhaps he heard the shouts because he wanted to believe that the bullets weren't real.

A second letter was from Hannah Chen of Jerusalem, and she succinctly summarized some of the most blatant suspicions of Roni Kempler.

- No one initially knew that he made the film, that a film of the assassination existed. Does that mean none of the security agents on the scene spotted him filming from a rooftop?
- And how did the video get to the media?
- Shouldn't the Shabak have confiscated the film from its owner, if this was the only documentary evidence describing the crime? And why didn't the filmmaker voluntarily turn over the film to the police?
- The film's authenticity is completely uncertain.
- In my opinion, it was tampered with. Perhaps people were removed or bullet sounds added. It appears to me that we were all fooled. The filmmaker worked for the Shabak, and everything to do with the film, and the timing of its release, was fake.

There were questions asked by the public. Why had Kempler waited almost two months to show the film when he would have been made rich had he sold it to the world networks the day following the assassination? In his sole television appearance on the night his film was broadcast, he answered the only way he could, he said he wasn't interested in making money.

Suspicious as its delayed appearance was, the film remains as valuable to solving the Rabin assassination as was the Zapruder film in the wake of the JFK murder.

In Kempler's film, the left back door of Rabin's supposedly empty vehicle closes before he enters. The Shamgar's Commission concluded that Rabin entered an empty car.

There is more from the Kempler film that contradicts the official findings; much more.

As the 15 minute film begins, Yigal Amir looks in the distance and, as a television commentator notes, "seems to be signaling someone." The possibility of an accomplice was noted at a Shamgar Commission hearing when police officers Boaz Eran and Moti Sergei testified that Amir spoke with a bearded man he appeared to know half an hour before the shooting.

One of the primary excuses given for not identifying Amir in the secured area was due to the crowds. To prove the point, police officers testified that "another well-known demonstrator, who works for the city, rushed at Rabin and shook his hand." Amir was not the only anti-Rabin individual in the sterile zone, but he stood for long minutes meters away from anyone else. No one could have missed him had they wanted to see him, Kempler's film certainly did not. Indeed, Amir was noticed when two security officers, strike up a conversation with him.

A few minutes later, Shimon Peres walks toward the crowd at the barrier, accepts their good wishes, and then walks to a spot about a meter and a half opposite the hood of Rabin's car. He is accompanied by four bodyguards, one of whom clearly points to Yigal Amir, sitting three meters away opposite them. Peres stops, looks inside the car, and begins a conversation with the bodyguards. All now take a good look at the windshield of Rabin's limousine, and then turn toward Amir.

At this point there is a cut in the video. Roni Kempler was asked to explain this under oath at Yigal Amir's trial. He testified, "Shimon Peres left and I filmed him as he was supposed to enter his car. But when Shimon Peres stood on the same spot for a long time, he stopped interesting me cinematically. I stopped filming and started again the moment he entered his car." But Peres is not walking to his car after the cut, but is seen talking to Rabin's driver, Menachem Damti. Damti was previously nowhere to be seen, and was most likely positioned at his post beside the driver's seat door.

Instead of getting into his car after a hard rally night and going home, Peres decided to examine Rabin's car and have a serious chat with the driver. Many seconds later, he started walking towards his own car. And yet, the true length of that conversation can't be known for a certainty due to the cut in the film.

Kempler's film continues as Peres enters his car and Rabin descends the steps. Strangely, the camera captures Rabin's rear bodyguard turning his head and stopping opposite Amir and Rabin, thus allowing Amir a clear shot at the Prime Minister. Amir draws his gun from deep inside his right pocket, and as the television commentator notes, "Amir is drawing his gun to shoot." Anyone, trained or not, could see that Amir was drawing a gun, and at that point he should have been pounced on. But, this was not to be. Instead, he circles student reporter Modi Yisrael, draws the gun and shoots.

Playing Kempler's video now frame-by-frame, we see that Rabin doesn't wince or flinch, though he had supposedly taken a hollow point nine mm bullet in his lung. He is not even pushed forward by the impact, nor does his suit exhibit signs of tearing. Instead, he continues walking forward and turns his head behind him, in the direction of the noise.

Three doctors watched this moment with me. Drs. B. and H. requested anonymity; Dr. Klein of Tel Aviv has no objection to being cited. I asked if Rabin's reaction was medically feasible if he was hit in the lung or if his backbone was shattered. I was told that if the spine was hit, Rabin would have fallen on the spot. However, in the case of a lung wound I was told that there are two types of pain reaction, one reflexive, the other delayed. Rabin, did not display the reflexive reaction, which would have most likely meant clutching the arm. Instead, he appeared startled, painlessly turning his head toward the direction of the shot. The conclusion of the doctors was that Rabin heard a shot, perhaps felt the blast of a blank and turned quickly towards the noise. This startled reaction does not occur simultaneously with a reflexive pain reaction.

Rabin takes one or two steps forward and suddenly the film becomes extremely hazy for two seconds. A well known Israeli camerman I have worked with is convinced the film was deliberately made fuzzy by an artificial process duplicating a sudden, quick movement of the camera. To illustrate this belief, he points out that white reflective light on the windshield stays in the same position while the camera is supposedly swishing.

The haze lifts momentarily almost two seconds later, and Rabin appears, still standing, but a step or two forward and somewhat to his right. It is at this point that we see that the entire conclusion of the Shamgar Commission was a lie. They told the public that after Amir first shot Rabin, Rabin's bodyguard fell on him, Amir was grabbed by two other bodyguards, but still managed to get closer to his quarry—shooting down, first at Rubin's elbow, then at Rabin's flank. But, the film shows Rabin standing, while Amir has disappeared from the screen. In just two seconds we see that Rubin did not jump on Rabin and Amir did not get closer to take two more shots on the prone bodyguard and Prime Minister. Then the swish returns and within the next moment of haze, another shot is heard but not seen.

Kempler told *Yediot Ahronot,* "The whole time I had the feeling that something bad would happen. There was anxiety in the air. Maybe because in the [army] reserves I deal in security, I am more sensitive to that."

Amir has said he was able to approach the Prime Minister by posing as a driver. Kempler said, "At first he looked suspicious to me as he sat by the plant ... he stood out, and with all the talk about political assassinations, attacks—he looked like a potential killer. Then I told myself that he was probably an undercover policeman, because otherwise the police would have dealt with him."

According to the testimony of bodyguard Yoram Rubin, as the shooting stops momentarily, he thinks to himself, "A defect in the weapon," and then according to Rubin, "I shouted at him several times, 'Yitzhak, can you hear me, just me and no one else, goddammit?' He [Rabin], helped me to my feet. That is, we worked together. He then jumped into the car. In retrospect, I find it amazing that a man his age could jump like that."

The Kempler film shows no jumping by either Rubin or Rabin. Furthermore, one famous photo shows that Rabin was pushed from the pavement into the car. Rubin's tale of athletic jumping is totally disproved by the video.

Then there is the issue of the back door of Rabin's limo closing before anyone was in the car. The Kempler film catches the flash of the famous photo of Rabin being pushed into the car over a second after the back door slams shut. This is proof positive that neither Rabin, Rubin, nor Damti were in the car yet, since Damti stays outside until after Rabin was placed in the vehicle. This segment has been examined and tested by numerous journalists, every shadow on the screen traced, every possible explanation exhausted, and in the end it has withstood all scrutiny. Someone was waiting inside the car for Rabin.

When I show this segment to audiences, inevitably I am asked, "Why did they make this film if it's so incriminating?" I reply, "The film convinced the whole country that Amir murdered Rabin. People always say, 'But, I saw him do it with my own eyes.' And that is what the film was supposed to do. But, the conspirators were so sloppy, they left in the truth. Either they didn't notice it, or they thought no one else would."

On the night his film was shown on Channel Two in January 1996, a fast-talking Kempler was obviously nervous when he was interviewed by commentator Rafi Reshef.

Reshef: "Why did you wait so long to release the film to the public?"
Kempler: "A few reasons. I didn't want to be known. Also, I thought it was forbidden to show the film so soon after the murder. The public needed time to digest it as a historic film ... But after the Shamgar Commission got it, I kept hearing on the street that I'm the sucker of the country. That really aggravated me, so I got a lawyer and decided to make some money selling it."

What Kempler didn't mention is that he hadn't told anyone he had filmed the assassination for two weeks. Later, realizing he had something important to offer the Shamgar Commission, he sent a registered letter informing them of the film's existence.

Reshef: "Did anyone observe you filming?"
Kempler: "Yes, the bodygua ... I'm sure I saw [singer] Aviv Gefen look right into my camera."

Kempler chose to not complete his original sentence, but this film shows it to be true when just before the Peres cut, one of his bodyguards turns back and looks directly up at Kempler. And yet, he changed his mind about this testimony.

Reshef: "Why did you concentrate so much of the film on the killer?"
Kempler: "I felt there was something suspicious about him. I let my imagination run away with me and felt murder in the air. It wasn't so strong when Peres was there, but when Rabin appeared, 'Wow.'"
Reshef: "There has been much speculation why you happened to be the only one in the right place to film the assassination. How do you explain it?"
Kempler: "I felt someone caused me to be in that place."
Reshef: "What, are you a fatalist? Did anyone try to interfere with you?"
Kempler: "There were undercover officers around. One told me it was alright to film, but I had to stop when Rabin appeared. An undercover policeman came up to me and asked me a few questions, and asked to see my ID. I showed it to him and he walked away. He stopped, turned back and shouted, 'What did you say your name was?' I shouted it back. He said, 'Good.' And that was that. The police had all the details of my identity."

What is described as a somewhat friendly encounter transformed at Amir's trial.

Kempler: "There was an undercover cop who told me not to film. I told him he had no right to tell me not to film. I asked him if something secret was going on? I told him again he had no right to tell me not to film. And if he does it again, I would take down his particulars and issue a complaint to the police."

A drastically altered situation.

Kempler: "When I stood on the balcony, I spent a lot of time in the dark, and to my regret, my imagination began to work overtime. I began to imagine many things, even God forbid, a political assassination ... I have no explanation why I had this feeling. I'm not sure it wasn't something mystic."

Kempler said he felt, "The defendant stood out. I don't know what he did ... but I recall he stood out. I can't recall anything other than what I filmed."

At the beginning of his testimony Kempler says the film shown to the public, "contained no changes or alterations." By the end, after Amir's attorney' persistant questions, he admitted, "There are gaps and there are differences."

Defense: "We don't hear everything in the film but we hear lots, including shouts. So why don't we hear the shouts of 'They're blanks?'"
Kempler: "Don't ask me. I'm not the address."
Defense: "Yoram Rubin testified that he fell on Rabin, why don't we see that in the film?"
Kempler: "I'm not a video or camera expert. I'm not the address for questions like that."

Yigal Amir was filmed a second time, during his reconstruction of the murder, several days after the event. This reconstruction at the crime scene deeply compromised the validity of the Kempler film.

The first error made was pointed out to me later by a man who claimed he was the first to report it to the press. In the reconstruction film, Amir shoots with his right hand, as numerous eye witnesses saw him do. But in the still of the Kempler film initially released exclusively to the newspaper *Yediot Ahronot,* Amir is shooting with his left hand.

And that's not all. A computerized comparison of the Kempler film and the *Yediot Ahronot* pictures reveal an entirely different face.

In the reconstruction film, Amir has bushy unshaped sideburns past the middle of his ear. The shooter in the Kempler photo still has squared sideburns at the top of his ear. Another person was super-imposed over Yigal Amir for the still and there is maybe one possible reason why. The superimposed figure's arm looks longer, thus reducing the range of the shot, a necessity to be explained shortly. This is just one possibility. There are others, so far, less convincing. Nonetheless, for whatever reason, Amir's image was almost certainly removed from the Kempler film still and replaced by another.

But the reconstruction film belied the Kempler film in other ways, as reluctantly testified to by Lieutenant Arieh Silberman, Amir's chief investigator, at the defendant's trial.

Defense: "Did you notice the differences between the video shown on Channel Two and the film of the reconstruction? Did you see the reconstruction film?"

Silberman: "I saw the reconstruction. It was of the same event in principle, but there was an obvious difference. You can see the difference."

Defense: "You're responsible for the defendant's investigation. Why is there a difference between the reconstruction film and the video shown on Channel 2?"

Silberman: "To my eyes, the difference isn't significant. The defendant doesn't think so. He never brought it up. I wasn't at the reconstruction."

Defense: "Why is there a break where we don't hear part of the audio?"

Silberman: "I didn't make the film. It was handled by the technicians of several units. I'm responsible for investigating the defendant, not the film."

Defense (Amir now acts as his own attorney): "Is there a difference between the original film and what was shown on Channel Two?"

Silberman: "Could be."

Defense: "What's the most outstanding difference?"

Silberman: "The position of the Prime Minister."

Defense: "In the reconstruction, I go straight toward him."

Silberman: "True."

Defense: "And in the original video I took a roundabout route."

Silberman: "According to what I saw, you circled someone before getting behind [Rabin]."

Amir reconstructed his alleged crime wrongly according to the Kempler film. And he shot with the wrong hand according to the still of the Kempler film. If Amir's attorneys had bothered to press the issue, they might have been able to constructed a plausible argument that he wasn't even at the scene of the crime.

Chapter Ten
THE PLOT BEGINS TO UNRAVEL

Blatant inconsistencies between the official version of the Rabin assassination and the truth finally clash publicly in October, 1996. Early in the month, *Maariv's* weekend magazine published a revealing collection of testimony I compiled from several policemen and security agents on duty at the assassination scene that fueled suspicions of a conspiracy from many formerly skeptical readers. On October 18, I was the victim of an eight minute hatchet job on Israeli Television Channel Two's weekend magazine program that was shown again the next night.

Despite the blatant attempt at character assassination, as *Yediot Ahronot* reported the Sunday following, I succeeded in igniting renewed national interest in the possibility that Rabin's murder was not as officially reported.

My appearance on national TV introduced to the Israeli public for the first time, proof that Rabin was shot in his car and not by Amir outside it. Even before the broadcast was finished, a phone threat arrived. The caller said, "Friend, you're going to leave the country. For you're own safety, you'd better leave the country." The same caller persisted for two days until I traced his phone number (he lived in Haifa) and complained to the police. The calls stopped and the police chose not to prosecute the culprit.

The Channel Two news team had deceived me, telling me they wanted to point out the inconsistencies of the Shamgar Commission when, in fact, their goal was to rush me through my own character assassination. Minutes after the report ended, three Labour Party politicians, including former Health Minister Ephraim Sneh, condemned my work. The news team itself arranged to have my lectures with two organizations canceled.

But the media is not the people. I was congratulated for my work by people wherever I went. My work, though labeled "radical," "extremist" and "inciteful" theory, was within six months accepted by many thousands of Israelis.

The *Maariv* report began with the issue of whether the bullets of the alleged assassin were real or not. It is not denied by the Shamgar Commission that "Blanks, blanks," was yelled by someone while Amir shot his weapon. The conclusion it reached is that Amir yelled it to confuse Rabin's bodyguards, a contention he denies. But, "Blanks, blanks" wasn't the only thing that was shouted.

S.G., Shabak Agent Under Command of Rabin's bodyguard Yoram Rubin: "I heard very clearly, 'They're not real, they're not real' during the shooting."

A.A., Personal Security Head of the Shabak: "I heard one shot and someone shouting, 'Not real, not real.' I can't say with certainty if it came from the shooter."

Avi Yahav, Tel Aviv policeman: "The shooter yelled, 'They're caps, nothing, caps.'"

None of the police or security men quoted by *Maariv* heard the famous 'Srak, srak,' (blanks, blanks) shout. The scene they describe is of a number of people shouting different phrases. What united the shouters was their belief that blank bullets were being shot.

Within four months, I had acquired the transcripts of Yigal Amir's trial and the police reports written on the night of the assassination. What they revealed was that a wide variety of shouts were heard including "They're caps," "They're dummy bullets," "It's a toy gun," and "Fake bullets." What follows is a sample of official testimony:

Menachem Damti, Rabin's Driver: "I heard the shooter shout, 'It's nothing.'"

Agent Sh.: "A policeman shouted, 'Calm down. They're blanks.'"
Policeman **Ephron Moshe:** "People yelled 'Blanks,' and 'Fake bullets.'"
Accused assassin **Yigal Amir:** "I shot and heard 'They're blanks,' from someone at the back, right side of the car."

How many bullets were shot? From *Maariv:*

A.H., Agent assigned to Yoram Rubin's staff: "I heard one shot, followed by another."
Maariv to **A.A.** (His name was later revealed as Adi Azoulai): "Are you certain you only heard one shot?"
A.A.: "Absolutely certain."
Avi Yahav: "I heard a number of shots. I'm not sure how many."
S.G.: "As I approached the car, I heard three shots."

From the trial and police records:

Yoram Rubin to the police investigator Yoni Hirshorn at 1:25, Nov. 5: "I heard three shots in a row." Yoram Rubin at Amir's trial: "I heard one shot, a pause and then two more shots."

Shabak agent **A.:** "I heard a shot, a pause, then another shot. Two shots, not in a row … The sound of the shots was different."
Policeman **Yisrael Gabai:** "There were three shots. The first one was followed by a pause, then two more in a row."
Policeman **Yamin Yitzhak:** "There were three shots in a row."
Agent Sh.: "I heard three shots but they didn't sound like normal shots. A policeman told me they were blanks."
Agent Ayin: "I heard one shot and then people shouting, 'It wasn't real.' I was interrogated by the Shabak before the police and I told both of them I only heard one shot."
Yigal Amir: "I paused between the first and second shots."
Policeman **Avi Yahav:** "I've been to countless target practices and this shot didn't sound like a gunshot. If it was a shot, it was a dud."
Police Officer **Moshe Ephron:** "I heard two shots but maybe there could have been three. The wall at Gan Ha'ir may have amplified the sound … The shots didn't sound natural. If they were real shots, they should have sounded much louder."

Police Officer **Shai Tiram**: "They didn't sound like normal shots, more like a firecracker than a gunshot. They weren't loud enough to be gunshots … The first shot sounded very different than the next two."

Policeman **Chanan Amram**: "It didn't sound like a gunshot, too quiet for that … First there was a pop noise, followed by another two."

Yoram Rubin: "The shots sounded real to me."

Police Officer **Yossi Smadja** to *Maariv* in July, 1996: "I'll swear I heard five shots, two clear and three muffled."

One policeman after another testified that he heard blanks or something other than a real bullet being fired. This is ample expert witness testimony that certainly suggests that Amir's bullets were, in fact, not real. But, how can one rationally explain the great variance in the number of shots heard? The Kempler film only shows Amir shooting once. A second shot is heard shortly after, but is not seen.

The inability of trained security and police personnel to agree on the number of shots is puzzling. But, on one issue all agree; none thought Rabin was hurt.

From *Maariv:*

Y.S., Shabak Head of Security for the Tel Aviv rally: "I heard Rabin was wounded only when I arrived at Ichilov Hospital some minutes later."

S.G.: "I didn't hear any cry of pain from the Prime Minister and didn't see any signs of blood whatsoever … It wasn't until some time after that I was told that Yoram Rubin was hurt."

Adi Azoulai: "Only after a number of inquiries as to whether Rabin was hurt, did I drive in shock to Ichilov."

From a police report on the night of the murder:

Agent Adi Azoulai: "I helped carry the Prime Minister into the car from the left. Yoram Rubin carried him from the right. We put him in the car and Rubin closed the door and the car left ... I wasn't certain if Rabin was hurt, so I phoned Ichilov to find out."

None of the security or police personnel detected any sign that Rabin was hurt, inexplicable for one shot in the lung and spleen by two hollowpoint 9 mm bullets. And a clip from Channel One's television coverage of the assassination night shows policemen searching the murder spot less than a half hour after the shooting. There is no blood on the pavement where Rabin fell. And again, recall Kempler's film of the assassination, which substantiates the witnesseses' testimony. After the blast from Amir's gun, Rabin is not pushed forward by the impact of the bullet, nor does he wince pain. Rather, he keeps on walking and turns his head quickly to his left.

Before examining the next issue in the *Maariv* article, let us skip to the report on my research on Channel Two. Despite the false allegations, one of my points came across loud and clear and kept my name from being totally besmirched. I showed the assassination film and pointed out that as Rabin entered his car, the opposite side passenger door was slammed shut. It was clear that the only way the door could be shut was if someone was inside the car shutting it. This was in direct contradiction to the Shamgar report which has Rabin and Rubin entering an empty back seat. The Kempler film shows both Rubin and Damti outside when the back door was slammed. Channel Two suggested the door was shut by the vibrations caused by Rabin's entrance. Throughout the country, people opened their back car doors and started shaking their vehicles. Nothing could make their doors shut. Furthermore, Rabin's door was armoured and 100 pounds more than the average car door. Add to the facts that the open front door of Rabin's car did not shut with the back, nor is any shaking of the vehicle in evidence on the film and you have someone, perhaps the real murderer, waiting for Rabin inside the car.

Six months later, radio announcer Razi Barkai attempted to justify Channel Two's explanation. He claimed to have phoned Cadillac headquarters and their spokesman explained that Cadillac doors are equipped with a special safety feature which automatically closes them when sudden pressure is applied to the seats.

This explanation does not stand up to scrutiny. A famous photo of Rabin being lifted into his car debunks Barkai's theory. The flash of this photo is recorded on the Kempler film after the door is well shut. Rabin was not even in the car yet to press on the seat and shut the magic door.

Yoram Rubin, Rabin's head of personal security. On November 8, 1995, was quoted as saying in the *New York Times* that Rabin's last words to him in the car were that he was hurt, but not seriously. He told the police on the night of the murder and later testified to the Shamgar Commission.

From *Maariv*:

Rubin to the Police from 1:07 AM, November 5, 1995: "I lifted the Prime Minister and pushed him into the car."

To the Shamgar Commission: "He [Rabin] helped me get up. That is to say, we worked together … We jumped, really jumped. I'm surprised, in retrospect, that a man his age could jump like that."

But, in the aforementioned photo, rubin is seen carrying Rabin into the car with Agent Azoulai. Carrying and jumping can't rationally be confused. Driver Menachem Damti also misrepresented his actions. *Maariv* reports Damti's police testimony: "I heard a shot and the shooter yell, "It's nothing, a blank." As soon as I heard the shot, I sat myself in the driver's seat, ready to go."

However, the Kempler film reveals that after the shot, Damti stayed outside and is filmed, apparently, helping to lift Rabin into the car.

The most disturbingly curious incident occured on the way to Ichilov Hospital, literally less than a minute's drive from the square. The trip took from 9:45 to just past 9:53. Damti was, quite possibly, the most experienced driver in the country. He had been the driver of every Prime Minister since 1974. But on the way to Ichilov he "became confused" and got lost. So after seven minutes of driving, Damti picked up policeman, Pinchas Terem, to help "direct" him to the hospital. How could Damti, who was a last minute replacement for Rabin's scheduled driver, accidentally get lost? The drive from Kings of Israel Square to Ichilov is straight and unhampered. Neither

Shimon Peres' nor Leah Rabin's drivers experienced any trouble speeding to their destinations. Damti took wrong turns though he should have known the correct route to Ichiliov by rote. He shouldn't have needed Officer Terem's help to find the hospital.

Terem got in the car and with the Prime Minister dying beside him, Yoram Rubin says to the new passenger, "I'm wounded, bandage me." As for Rabin, we can only guess that Rubin didn't care that his wounds needed much more urgent attention. Terem completed his bizarre testimony by noting that Damti did not notify Ichilov by radio that he was coming and thus the hospital staff was totally unprepared for Rabin's arrival.

Someone in the Shabak certainly should have informed Ichilov by radio that Rabin was coming, but did not. And Damti should have radioed that he was lost, but did not. When the hapless adventure ended finally at the gates of Ichilov Hospital, the security guard would not permit the Prime Minister's vehicle to enter. He registered the vehicle as arriving at just past 9:53 and Damti and Terem went scrambling out of the car looking for a stretcher and some help. Rabin entered the hospital eventually; but no one, though reporters were there, ever saw or filmed him being admitted through the main outpatient's clinic of Ichilov.

Rabin's unpained demeanor (non-injured state) after the shots, the unexplained limousine door, and the unusually long drive to the hospital, all do more than suggest that Rabin was unhurt by Amir's blank bullets and was shot inside the car. It certainly appears that Rubin took a harmless arm wound to cover his role in the event, and Damti picked up a policeman as a witness in case of future disbelief.

Chapter Eleven
LEAH RABIN'S CONFUSING NIGHT

On March 28, 1997, *Yediot Ahronot* published an excerpt from Leah Rabin's book about husband Yitzhak's assassination. What follows is her version of the events of the fateful night of November 4, 1995 translated from the original Hebrew.

"On the way to the rally, Yoram Rubin [Rabin's personal bodyguard] turned his head and in a threatening voice reported, 'Yitzhak, I want to inform you that we have a serious warning about the possibility of a suicide bomber tonight at the rally. Perhaps a terrorist will infiltrate the square tonight.'"

"At the rally, the wife of a *Haaretz* reporter asked me if Yitzhak was wearing a bulletpoof vest. Yitzhak would never wear a bulletproof vest on an occasion like this."

No bulletproof vest when a serious possibility of a suicide bomber was reported to him by his personal bodyguard? What kind of a bodyguard would not insist that the Prime Minister wear a protective jacket, whether he liked it or not, in the face of mortal danger?

"We began to descend the steps, me one step behind him. Shimon Peres, I learned later, considered waiting for Yitzhak to exchange a few words but decided to do so at another opportunity. I was still on the steps while Yitzhak was already beside the car. The driver Damti waited beside his door in order to help him enter the car."

In the Kempler film of the assassination, Peres is seen awaiting something, but if it is Rabin, he's on the wrong side of the car. A significant cut in the film occurs when Peres waits opposite Rabin's car. Damti appears after the cut standing beside Peres, talking to him; he is nowhere near the door Rabin is supposed to enter. Leah Rabin is mistaken on these points.

"I heard three blasts. Suddenly I stood alone and someone shouted, 'This wasn't real!' After that, a second bodyguard pushed me into the next car in line. It was the same bodyguards' car that accompanied us from our home to the rally. The Cadillac already pulled away slowly with Yitzhak, the driver Damti and the bodyguard Yoram Rubin inside.

"The car I sat in then pulled away, past the crowds and into the street, not stopping for red lights. 'Where are we going?' I thought. I didn't see the Cadillac or any security vehicles. I didn't think the guys knew where they were going. Over and over I asked them, 'What happened?' and each time they answered me, 'It wasn't real.'

"'What wasn't real?' There was no answer. Were they just repeating what we all heard at the rally or things they were told through their earphones? The bodyguards were silent and obviously obeying orders given to them. I recalled Yitzhak being covered by bodyguards. There was a threat and they protected him. When I last stared at Yitzhak, before he disappeared under the bodyguards, he looked just fine."

The last observation confirms that of numerous witnesses who saw Rabin survive the shot(s) without any sign of physical pain. The same observation is confirmed by the Kempler film which shows Rabin healthily walking forward after the first and only shot recorded on the film.

"According to our plans, we were supposed to go to a party in Tzahala. I realized we were travelling in the wrong direction. 'Why are we going this way?' I asked. 'It's the wrong way.' There was no answer. "Where is Yitzhak?" the words popped out of me. 'If this wasn't real, where is Yitzhak?' 'In the second car,' the bodyguards answered. 'Where?' 'Behind us.' 'In what car?' I didn't see any car. 'In what car?' I asked again. Finally they told the truth. 'We don't know.'

"I asked myself why none of them tried to clear up matters by radio. This was very strange. Today I think they were ordered to maintain radio silence to prevent us being located. "Where are we going," I asked. 'To Shabak headquarters,' I was told. I entered a modest room and was told to sit beside a table and wait. 'When we know something, we'll tell you,' said one of the Shabak agents.

"The moments passed slowly and I began to think the bullets might not have been blanks. Young Shabak personnel went in and out of the room. 'What happened to him?' I asked ceaselessly. 'Don't worry,' I was told. 'When we know something, we'll tell you.'

"I'm not used to waiting but the personnel had no information. They did not treat me with friendliness or rudeness ... Two sentences finally penetrated my ear: 'One hurt seriously, the other lightly.'

"'Where is he?' I asked. They finally admitted, 'At Ichilov.' It had already been twenty minutes since we arrived and if Yitzhak was seriously wounded, they would have told me. But they didn't say a word. 'Take me to Ichilov,' I demanded."

The story, needless to say, is bizarre. In what other political assassination, or mere murder, was the wife told repeatedly by different bodyguards that the shooting wasn't real? The only possible reason for these assertions was that the bodyguards were told an exercise was going to take place. This is what the bodyguards probably thought had happened, and this is what was told to Leah Rabin.

Why was Leah Rabin separated from her husband on the steps

and later escorted into a separate car full of bodyguards who seemed to be waiting for her and knew exactly where to take her, seconds after the shooting? How curious that Leah Rabin's movements could be so well choreographed while her husband's were so botched. More to the point, why wasn't she taken to Ichilov Hospital to join her husband?

The Prime Minister's car departed at 9:45 PM for the one-minute trip to the hospital, but arrived eight minutes later at 9:53 PM. The given reason for Yitzhak Rabin's late arrival was that the crowd prevented a quick exit. This problem, however, did not detain Leah Rabin's vehicle in the same way it did her husband's limousine. Yitzhak Rabin's driver, Menachem Damti, drove down back roads until he got "lost."

How can one explain the absolutely shabby treatment accorded the wife of the Prime Minister by the Shabak agents? Why did the bodyguards in the car lie to her about her husband's condition? Why did they ignore her legitimate inquiries? Why didn't they use the car radio to keep her informed? Why were they so dishonest with her at Shabak headquarters?

Chapter Twelve
THE TESTIMONY OF CHIEF LIEUTENANT BARUCH GLADSTEIN: AMIR DIDN'T SHOOT RABIN

Everyone who saw the Kempler video of the assassination of Yitzhak Rabin saw Yigal Amir shoot the Prime Minister from a good two feet behind him. The conclusion of the Shamgar Commission was that Amir shot Rabin in the back twice: first in the upper back from some 50 cm distance and then in the lower back while standing 30 cm above him. The commission also found that Amir shot bodyguard Yoram Rubin in the elbow from about 30 cm above him.

Now, consider the testimony of Chief Lieutenant Baruch Gladstein of Israel Police's Materials and Fibers Laboratory, given at the trial of Yigal Amir on January 28, 1996.

Gladstein: "I serve in the Israel Police Fibers and Materials Laboratory. I presented my professional findings in a summation registered as Report 39/T after being asked to test the clothing of Yitzhak Rabin and his bodyguard Yoram Rubin with the aim of determining the range of the shots.

"I would like to say a few words of explanation before presenting my findings. We reach our conclusions after testing materials microscopically, photographically and through sensitive chemical and technical procedures. After being shot, particles from the cartridge are expelled through the barrel. They include remains of burnt carbon, lead, copper and other metals.

"The greater the distance of the shot, the less the concentration of the particles and the more they are spread out. At point blank range, there is another phenomenon, a characteristic tearing of the clothing and abundance of gunpowder caused by the gases of the cartridge having nowhere to escape. Even if the shot is from a centimeter, two or three, you won't see the tearing and abundance of gunpowder. These are evident only from point blank shots.

"To further estimate range, we shoot the same bullets, from the suspected weapon under the same circumstances. On May 11, 1995, I received the Prime Minister's jacket, shirt and undershirt, as well as the clothes of bodyguard Yoram Rubin including his jacket, shirt and undershirt. In the upper section of the Prime Minister's jacket I found a bullethole to the right of the seam, which according to my testing of the spread of gunpowder, was caused by a shot from less than 25 cm range. The same conclusion was reached after testing the shirt and undershirt.

"The second bullethole was found on the bottom left hand side of the jacket. It was characterized by a massed abundance of gunpowder, a large quantity of lead, and a 6 cm. tear, all the characteristics of a point blank shot."

Lest anyone miss the significance of the testimony, Chief Lieutenant Gladstein testified that the gun which killed Rabin was shot first from less than 25 cm range, and then the barrel was placed directly on his body. In fact, according to trial witness, Nathan Gefen, Gladstein said the gun was initially shot 10 cm away, and such was originally typed into court records. (Known as Protocols in Israel.) The number 25 was crudely written atop the original 10.

If the shots that killed Rabin were from point blank range and 25 cm distance Amir couldn't have shot them.

"As to the lower bullethole, according to the powder and lead formations and the fact that a secondary hole was found atop the main entry hole, it is highly likely that the Prime Minister was shot while bending over. The angle was from above to below. I have photographs to illustrate my conclusions."

The court was now shown photographs of Rabin's clothing. According to the Shamgar Commission, Rabin was shot first standing up and then shot again while covered by Yoram Rubin's body prone on the ground. Nowhere else but in Gladstein's expert testimony, is there so much as a hint that he was shot while in a bent-over position.

"After examing the bullethole in the sleeve of Yoram Rubin, I determined that the presence of copper and lead, plus the collection of gunpowder leads to the likelihood that he, too, was shot from near point blank range. The presence of copper means the bullet used to shoot Rubin was different from that found in the Prime Minister's clothing which was composed entirely of brass. The bullet that was shot at Rubin was never found."

We now enter the realm of the bizarre, when Yigal Amir chooses to cross-examine a witness. After Chief Lieutenant Gladstein provides proof that Amir did not shoot the bullets that killed Rabin, Amir is determined to undermine the testimony.

Amir: "According to your testimony, I placed the gun right on his back."

Gladstein: "You placed the gun on his back on the second shot and fired."

Amir: "And the first shot was from 50 cm?"

Gladstein: "Less than 20 cm."

Amir: "If one takes into account that there is more gunpowder from the barrel, then the muzzle blast should also increase."

Gladstein: "To solve this problem, I shot with the same ammunition, and in your case, from the same gun. I shot the Beretta 9 mm weapon with hollowpoint bullets into the Prime Minister's jacket."

Amir: "When I took the first shot, I saw a very unusual blast."

Amir was likely coming to the conclusion that he shot a blank bullet, but changes direction when he concluded, "We need a new expert. I didn't shoot from point blank range." The Materials and Fibers Laboratory of Israel Police concludes that Rabin was shot from less than 20 cm, and from point blank range, no matter what Amir or the video says. Furthermore, bodyguard Yoram Rubin was shot by a different bullet than the kind that felled Rabin or was even found in Amir's clip. Unless Israel Police's fibers expert is deliberately promoting far-right, conspiracy nut theories, Yigal Amir's gun did not kill Yitzhak Rabin.

Chapter Thirteen
KANGAROO COURT

Amir's lawyers seem conflicted about his case. At first, attorneys Gabi Shahar, Jonathan Goldberg, and Shmuel Fleishmann were forthcoming with information. Fleischmann admitted to NBC *Extra* that, "We are looking at Dallas and JFK all over again." Shahar was also convinced that his client was a victim of a conspiracy. Today both lawyers insist Amir got what he deserved.

Jonathan Goldberg wrote a long article outlining a conspiracy for a British magazine, but when I requested an interview with him, his researcher Mordechai Sones arrived at my home instead, with little new information.

It's far from unlikely that Goldberg was told to clam up. In April 1997, I received a letter from a friend of attorney Goldberg, postmark from Tsfat, that informed me, "Mr. Goldberg was in the process of co-writing a book on the Rabin murder with an American intelligence writer when threats forced him to stop the project." I contacted the letter writer and admit I cannot completely vouch for his message. However, I estimate odds are it is more likely true than not.

The truth of what happened at Amir's trial was not revealed publicly by the lawyers involved, and seemed it never would be. But on May 27, 1997, I was faxed an interview with Gabi Shahar published just after Amir's trial, in the Russian-language newspaper *Vesti,* translated into Hebrew. This obscure interview, at last, revealed the true nature of the battle the attorneys faced.

Vesti: "You agreed to represent Amir despite the fact that one lawyer after another refused to be appointed on moral grounds."

Shahar: "I took on the case on February 1, 1996, two days after Judge Edmund Levi asked me to handle the defense of Yigal Amir. My only condition was the defendant's consent, which I received. I was the third attorney appointed by the state and was given no preparatory material. I sat in my first court meeting without any preparation."

Vesti: "You took on a client who had confessed and was cooperating fully with the authorities. So what was the function of a defense?"

Shahar: "After reading the material in the file, I discovered many unanswered questions that the prosecution had not replied to satisfactorily. First of all, I noticed the following fact: In the prosecution's version, Yigal Amir shot three bullets from a Baretta 9 mm gun. The first hit the Prime Minister's back. The expert from the Israel Police's Criminal Investigations Laboratory tested the Prime Minister's clothes and determined that the bullet came from 25 cm distance. In the video taken by Kempler, we all see the shot came from well over 50 cm distance. But let's talk about the third bullet. The tests show Rabin was shot in the lower portion of the back and the bullet's path was up/down. Yet, the police's ballistics expert testified that this bullet was shot from point blank. When I asked him about his findings in court, the expert testified that the bullet wasn't shot from even 2 or 3 cm's distance, rather point blank. But consider that after Rabin took the first bullet, he was felled and was already lying on the asphalt during the shooting of the third bullet. Amir, under no circumstances, could have shot point blank."

Not one witness testified in court that, after the first shot, Amir managed to get close enough to shoot another round from zero range. To the contrary, everyone testified that immediately after the first shot, policemen, bodyguards and Shabak agents pounced on Amir. Logic dictates that the distance between Amir and Rabin widened considerably after the first shot.

Vesti: "Did the defense organize a pathological examination?"

Shahar: "No. Not one known expert agreed to conduct a pathological examination, and the court turned down our request for funding to pay for the examination."

Shahar's revelation is astounding. No independent examination of Rabin's body was ever undertaken. There was no autopsy. The only proof of what happened to the body is found in the muddled and contradictory reports from Ichilov Hospital on the night of the murder. By the morning, Rabin's body was transferred from the privately-run Ichilov to the state-run Tel Hashomer Hospital.

Vesti : "In his files are other inconsistencies. For instance, the police ballistics expert testified that there were eight bullets left in Amir's clip. Another policeman testified that he had removed a ninth bullet from the chamber of Amir's gun. Yigal Amir testified on numerous occasions that he had loaded nine bullets and eight were still in his gun. A question; who shot at least two more rounds? Perhaps Amir is lying."

Shahar: "What for? From the first moment, Amir has consistently stood on his guilt, revealing his act in great detail. On the night of the murder, his police interrogation was recorded on videotape."

Vesti interrupts to note that Israel's infamous police minister, Moshe Shahal, was also filmed in Amir's interrogation room, a fact that is probably very important.

Shahar: "Yigal Amir not only confessed to the act, he boasted that he fulfilled his criminal goal. He had no desire to lie or deny anything. As a former investigator with years of experience, I know that the interrogator must collect testimony with complete accuracy or it won't stand up in court. During the first session, the investigator asked Yigal Amir, 'How many bullets were in the clip?' He replied, 'Nine, I'm not sure, but the clip wasn't full.'"

"How many shots did you fire?" asked the investigator.

"Three," answered Amir.

"Where are the rest of the bullets?" asked the investigator in astonishment. He also understood from the beginning that there was a huge contradiction between the police report and what Amir was saying.

"You originally said there were nine bullets in your clip," Amir is asked.

"True."

"Does it hold nine or fourteen?"

"The clip holds thirteen bullets."

"With the possibility of loading a fourteen into the chamber?"

"No, actually, yes, yes. But I wouldn't have done that," answered Amir.

"Then by simple calculation, we're missing a few bullets," observed the investigator. "Are you saying you arrived with nine bullets?"

"I didn't fill the clip."

If we believe Amir's testimony, after he shoots three times and a policeman removes one bullet from the gun, there should have been five bullets left in the clip, not eight.

Vesti: "How many bullets can fit into the Baretta's clip?"

Shahar: "Thirteeen bullets in theory, but Amir was superstitious and according to his mystical theory, which he presented to the court, if God wanted Rabin to die, two bullets were enough."

Vesti: "How did the judges respond to your line of reasoning?"

Shahar: "The judges called a halt to the proceedings immediately after they heard me. I had the feeling the judges couldn't answer my questions. The judges began a series of criticisms against me. Later, when I presented the evidence of contradictions in the number of bullets from police files, they refused to hear my arguments."

Vesti: "Did you try and arrange independent ballistics tests?"

Shahar: "Of course. But the judges turned down our request, claiming too much time had already been wasted on the investigation."

In the court transcripts, is the testimony of Shabak agent B.L. (Benny Lahav), who received a letter of warning from the Shamgar Commission that he was liable for prosecution. He had demanded, in no uncertain terms, that the policeman who picked up Amir's gun hand it over to him. The demands were so intimidating that the policeman contacted his superior, the head of the Yarkon police division, to protect him. He succeeded and the police maintained possession.

Incidentally, there was a good opportunity to compare the ballistics report in a different way; by examining Yoram Rubin's wounds when he was in the hospital. This wasn't done by the prosecution or the defense.

In short, attorney Shahar suspects that Rabin and Rubin were shot by a gun that wasn't Amir's. The Shabak agent, Benny Lahav, head of VIP Protection, was desperate to get possession of Amir's gun before police did. After it was in the Shabak's possession, any replacement and adjustments could have been made. But the police kept the gun and their ballistics tests threw the Shabak's story to the wind. The court refused to allow independent pathological and ballistics tests. No court pathologist examined bodyguard Yoram Rubin's wound to see if it matched Amir's gun, even though evidence did show his wound came from a different type of bullet. When Shahar insisted on expounding on the significance of the contradictory bullets testimony, the judges called a recess and later roundly condemned him for his "speculations." The kangaroo court was in full swing.

Shahar: "The prosecution took another route. Instead of examing Rubin by an expert pathologist, they gathered suitable reports from Ichilov and passed them on to the court. But, within one report by Dr. Hamo who treated Rubin, is his supposition that Rubin was shot twice. He wrote among other things, 'A bodyguard, about 30 years old, arrived at the hospital with two bullet wounds in his left arm.' I'm prepared to accept that one bullet caused two wounds but that had to be checked by an expert and it never was."

Another inconsistency occurred when Yoram Rubin appeared in court on his own volition before the trial began and changed his testimony. He then testified, "That it was said there were four to five bullets is wrong. I testify that there were three bullets shot." But no one had ever asked Rubin how many bullets were shot.

Vesti: "How do you explain Rubin's 'initiative?'"
Shahar: "As a former police investigator I'd say Rubin was terrified that he'd get the blame since he was responsible for Rabin's life. After I discovered this, I decided to question Rubin in indirect cross-examination."

Vesti: "What's the difference between direct cross-examination and indirect cross-examination?"

Shahar: "In direct cross-examination, I respond to questions posed by the prosecution. The prosecution, however, did not ask Rubin about the number of shots. But Rubin testified to a different number in his police investigation than to the court. In the course of the indirect cross-examination, I asked Rubin how many shots he heard. He avoided a direct answer. Finally, he said that while in hospital a friend told him there were four or five. As a legalist, I couldn't accept this explanation.

"In other words, the court claimed the following: Bullets pulled out of Rabin matched Amir's gun, so why are you pursuing new evidence? But, let's look at what happened to the bullets from the crime scene *en route* to the police laboratory. The pathologist Yehuda Hiss testified that the bullets were transferred to a safe in the Legal Medicine Institute. He doesn't testify who transferred them or when, though both facts, according to the law, must be registered.

"The bullets were removed from the body of the deceased at about 2 a.m. at Ichilov Hospital. The Institute transferred them to the Crime Identification Laboratory of Central Police Headquarters at 12 noon the next day. Who took the bullets to the police headquarters at Abu Kabir? Who delivered them to the Criminal Investigation laboratory? Talk about breaking the chain of evidence!

"In court I stressed that the prosecution had not proved that the bullets tested by the police laboratory were the same bullets removed from Rabin. The judge replied, 'Why are you bringing up this evidence when the defendant has already stubbornly confessed that it was he who did the shooting?'"

"For example, imagine this: we accuse someone of drug selling on the basis that a plastic bag of dope had his fingerprints on it. But the investigator did not register the bag as evidence, so the accused is released for lack of evidence. In every legal hearing, once there are holes in the chain of evidence, all responsibility falls on the prosecution and not the defense. In this criminal case, most of the burden of proof fell on the defense.

No one could account for the whereabouts of the bullets pulled out of Rabin's body for a full eleven hours. The chain of evidence was clearly broken. One attorney told me that Amir's case would have been thrown out of most American courts. There was no legal physical evidence linking him to the crime."

The bullets that the public saw in newspaper photos were in noticeably fine shape considering that hollowpoints are supposed to expand and shatter upon impact. To one police medic, the whole issue of hollowpoint bullets is illogical. She told me, 'Yigal Amir's brother Hagai was convicted of hollowing out the bullets. Why would he need to? Hollowpoints are legal in Israel and can be purchased as easily as regular bullets. Why hollow them out when Yigal Amir or his brother could have just bought them?' "

Vesti: "How did the court react to your line of questions?"
Shahar: "After presenting my assumptions about the internal contradictions within Amir's case, the court rejected them all."
Vesti: "What did you base your theory on?"
Shahar: "Simple. Yigal Amir was most energetic in his desire to be convicted of the murder of the Prime Minister. Thus, he had no interest in lying or obfuscating to prove the opposite. The paradox is that during the hearing, Amir himself began to acquire doubts."
Vesti: "What were Yigal Amir's doubts?"
Shahar: "About a few things. He was genuinely shocked when, as he was shooting, someone yelled, 'They're not real. They're blank bullets.'"
Vesti: "And what happened in court?"

Before he answered the question, Shahar quoted a *Yediot Ahronot* report by Yael Horovitz which read, "A group of people very near the Prime Minister heard the cries, 'Blanks, blanks.' A right wing source says he heard the cries from one of the bodyguards."

Shahar: "Now let's examine Amir's police interrogation as recorded by the court transcripts."
Investigator: "As far as I understand, you waited and prepared yourself for this?"
Amir: "Don't know … I'll tell you there were strange things. Maybe you won't believe me, but to this day I didn't know I was going to kill Rabin. That is to say, I said to myself if there's an opportunity. I stood there and watched, I stood there among them for 50 minutes and no one said a thing."

Investigator: "What do you mean 'among them?' Among who?"

Amir: "Among the police and bodyguards."

Investigator: "Among the police and bodyguards?"

Amir: "There are things that are … [deleted from the transcript]. They yelled, 'It's a blank.'"

Investigator: "You don't think that was a screw-up, that the guards didn't function correctly?"

Amir: "What do you mean? Why did they have to shout, 'It's a blank bullet?' Would a bodyguard watching the Prime Minister get shot really shout, 'They're blank bullets?'"

Investigator: "That is strange."

Shahar: "The judge asked me, 'Are you implying that Amir didn't shoot Rabin? Then whose bullets did?' I answered him like this: 'Someone who knew ahead of time that blank bullets were being fired could have exploited the opportunity. He wouldn't have to be a government representative. Anyone who knew beforehand that blanks were going to be fired could have wounded the Prime Minister with a silencer on his gun.

"To my great sorrow, the court not only refused to consider the doubts raised by the defense but condemned us for implying that there could be any doubt."

Vesti: "Did the court hear the testimony of Avishai Raviv, the Shabak agent code named 'Champagne?'" He befriended Amir and was held by the police briefly after the assassination, then released.

Shahar: "No, Raviv didn't appear in court. On a number of occasions I tried to contact him to be a witness for Amir. With great difficulty I found his cell phone number but he pointedly refused to speak to me. Time after time someone else answered, calling himself a bodyguard or friend of Raviv's."

Vesti: "Many have claimed that Raviv provoked Amir into action constantly. He was head of Eyal which publicized its existence on television. Wasn't the court obliged to have him testify and shed light on matters?"

Shahar: "All the police files against Raviv disappeared, over 15 of them. The one document revealing Raviv's criminal past that was presented to the court was done so in secret session."

Vesti: "What was the general reaction to your defending Yigal Amir?"

Shahar: "Much milder than I would have guessed. Some people tried to talk me out of it but many others sent me faxes with theories and proofs of their own. For example, one woman wrote that the man who they said videoed the murder [Roni Kempler] wasn't the same man who appeared in court."

As wild as the woman's accusation sounds, the fact is that Kempler seemed to be a last minute replacement for another "filmmaker." When the amateur film was first announced, the name of the filmmaker released to the media was not Kempler, rather, a Polish tourist with a lengthy unpronounceable name, long forgotten. Someone thought the better of using him and instead, Roni Kempler got his fifteen minutes of fame ... literally; he hasn't been heard from since.

Avishai Raviv, the most relevant witness of all, was not called to testify, nor apparently was Shahar given subpoena privileges to force him to be a witness for the defense, hostile or not. Without Raviv on the stand, the court denied Amir any chance of a fair trial and prevented the Israeli public from hearing the truth about the murder of their Prime Minister.

Shahar describes a trial in which no evidence contrary to the established version of events could be presented, no counter scenarios vocalized, and no confusing testimony discussed. The court found no money or desire to organize the most basic pathological and ballistics tests. Of course the idea was to give him a trial and prove to the nation and the world that there is justice in Israel. But, Shahar's description of the legal proceedings paints a very different portrait of justice in Israel.

Chapter Fourteen
YORAM RUBIN, LIAR

Following is information formerly withheld from the media and public. It is the testimony of Yitzhak Rabin's personal bodyguard Yoram Rubin taken from the secret transcripts of the trial of Yigal Amir.

The secret testimony begins with the court asking Rubin why the session should be closed. Rubin replied, "I don't mind being photographed, but within my story I could touch on matters that I wouldn't want made public."

A representative of the intelligence services then explained that operating procedures and details of secret servicemen should not be publicized. The defense argued that the court could decide whether to proceed after hearing its questions. This argument did not sway the judges and they decided to hold the session in camera and afterwards sign a declaration that they heard testimony denied the public.

The final declaration of the three judges; Levi, Rothlevy, and Mordick, read that, "To prevent speculation, we must relate that the previous testimony was held behind closed doors, is not for public attention, and will not be included in the trial transcripts."

In one of the most bizarre episodes of the trial, Amir acted as his own attorney and personally questioned Rubin, one of the two men he allegedly shot.

Rubin first testified that seven bodyguards in two groups covered Rabin. He was then asked by Amir why Rabin didn't wear a bulletproof vest. He answered, "We judge the situation and decide if a bulletproof vest is called for. Vests are worn only in exceptional cases. The bodyguards never wear them." At this point Rubin makes a rather remarkable statement. "There were previous warnings that an incident could happen."

Needless to say, if there were prior warnings, then it was up to Rubin to make certain Rabin was wearing a bulletproof vest. Amir did not jump on this point, rather he returned to the question of the makeup of Rabin's bodyguard formation.

Amir: "You pointed out that seven bodyguards surrounded Rabin."
Rubin: "There were seven attached to him and twenty in all. I was the commander of one group, I walked beside him, another preceded him, another man walked behind him and he was joined by someone to the left, they formed the pair guarding the rear. One other proceeded forward and another right to cover the fence on Ibn Gvirol Street."
Amir: "You were with Rabin on the left side."

Rubin: "No. I didn't walk on his left."

Amir now questioned the security arrangements but did not make his point. Instead, he digressed, asking questions about whether bulletproof vests can be discerned under clothing. His attorney, Jonathan Goldberg, addressed Rubin to help get Amir back on the right track.

Defense: "Was the protective ring around Rabin different at this rally than at other events. Because according to the defendant, he circled the Prime Minister and saw that his protective guard was different."
Rubin: "It was different."
Defense: "The defendant says that at prior events the formation was two bodyguards on the side, one in front and another in back but this time the formation was different."
Amir: "At the rally when I got into Rabin's range, a hole opened up for me, I walked around someone and came in from the side. I always wanted to kill Rabin but I didn't believe that I'd ever have room to push my hand right to him. But that's what happened in this case. When I walked towards him I saw a gap open and I shot him in the back."

In this round, he admits to murdering Rabin but has planted deep suspicions that he had help from Rubin and other Shabak agents. He stops just short of saying he couldn't have done it without their help. Of course, the judges didn't see it that way. But any other objective observer would ask why Rabin wasn't wearing a bulletproof vest if warnings against his life were received, why the bodyguards changed their regular formation that night and how did they allow the gap to open which permitted Amir an unhampered shot at the Prime Minister?

In Rubin's statement to the police investigator Yoni Hirshorn on the night of the murder he said:

Rubin: "There were three shots in a row ... I picked up Rabin and threw him in the car. I lay him on the seat and asked him if he was shot. He told me he thought so but not too badly ... He lost consciousness and I quickly attempted to revive him..."

Compare this with his testimony at Amir's trial. Rubin was on the stand twice. We will begin with his testimony given on January 29, 1996.

Rubin: "On April 11, 1995, I was the Prime Minister's bodyguard. We descended the steps, and for tactical reasons I moved half a step right toward the crowd, thinking Yitzhak was going there to shake hands. Suddenly, he changed his mind and walked left toward the car. In principle we were supposed to get in the far right back door but we never got there."

According to Rubin, it was Rabin himself who changed directions. That lets him off the hook for not spotting Amir or covering Rabin in time. He was going right, while Rabin altered the route and turned left. Hence, he was out of position to protect Rabin just at the moment Amir shot. Rubin also begins his testimony with a plausible explanation of why the right back door was open... though he does not dare try to explain why it shut from the inside before he, the driver or Rabin were in the car.

Rubin: "As he turned left and we were opposite the back door on the driver's side, I heard a shot from 45 degrees behind me to the left. At this point I doubted that it was a gunshot. Then I realized, it was a shot. I grabbed Yitzhak and covered him. At this point we fell down. Now I felt a hit in my shoulder area like a jolt of electricity and I heard a third shot. We continued lying on the ground. I wish to stress the following points. I grabbed [Rabin] with both hands. As I lay on his back a bullet entered my elbow and exited the armpit ... I have no doubt that there were three shots not four or five like it was said. There was a gap between the first and second shot. This gave me time to cover the Prime Minister. Then came two quick shots, one after another. I noticed there was a hiatus in the shooting and I thought to myself that there was a defect in the weapon or that the shooter was apprehended. I grabbed Rabin by the shoulders, I told him, 'Do you hear me, just me and no one else?' This I shouted. 'Goddamit, do you hear me?' I repeated several times. Then there was a period I don't recall and I found myself on top of him in the car. Damti drove us to Ichilov for medical treatment. The ride, I estimate took a minute and a half, but I'm not sure. I was in the hospital for five days according to the newspapers. Now I'm alright."

What he forgets is most fortuitous for him. He had previously testified to the Shamgar Commission that Rabin was alive after the shots. Not just alive: "He helped me get up. Then we jumped. In retrospect I'm amazed that a man his age could jump like that ... We jumped into the car, he on the seat, me between the seats. Both our legs were dangling outside. I put his in, then mine and told Damti to get moving."

The ride took a minute and a half? Not according to the driver or to Ichilov records. It took just over eight minutes. And fully conscious with a wound to the arm, he didn't remember how many days he was in the hospital? Instead, he relied on the newspapers to remind him.

Rubin: "I didn't see the defendant ... I stood behind and to the right of the Prime Minister. To his left another person walked in front [of Amir]. He wasn't the one they arrested, they arrested the one behind him."

Rubin didn't see Amir but he got a good look at a person walking to his left ahead of him. If he didn't see Amir, how did he know the other person was walking in front of him and to the left?

Rubin: "I heard people saying the bullets were blanks. I don't know who said this. They said the gun was a fake or the bullets were blanks, I'm not sure which version is right and it doesn't interest me. I didn't think the bullets were blanks, I felt they weren't blanks. The first shot also didn't sound real. But you don't take chances."

Defense: "Peres and Rabin descended the steps separately. Don't they usually descend together?"
Prosecution: "Objection. We know what happened."
Court: "Objection sustained."
Defense: "Was there a difference in the sound between the first bullet and the last two?"

Rubin: "Yes. After the first shot, I jumped on him and we fell together to the ground. I spoke to Yitzhak and we jumped into the car."
Defense: "Did you hear the shout of "They're blanks" during the gap between the first and second shots?"
Rubin: "No, at the end."

We will never know why Rabin and Peres did not descend the steps together as was the custom, but we can see that Rubin's testimony was unravelling. Instead of the blank spot in his memory between the time of the shots and finding himself in the car, Rubin's memory returns and he recalls jumping into the car with Rabin; an event the Kempler film proves didn't happen and which contradicts his statement to the police that he tossed Rabin into the car. And the Kempler film shows that after the first shot, Rubin did not immediately jump on Rabin. Instead Rabin kept walking. The film never shows Rubin felling Rabin. His memory deeply failed him on another issue as well: just minutes before, he testified that he heard the "Blanks" shout after the first shot, now it's after the third.

Rubin's second round of testimony in the Amir trial was on April 3, 1996. During the interim, testimony of other witnesses put Rubin's version of events in deep jeopardy.

According to Rubin, he was lying on the ground atop Rabin when he was shot through the elbow and the bullet exited his armpit. Other Shabak officers and one policeman, Yisrael Gabai, testified that Amir was being held while standing and he shot his last two bullets downward at Rubin and Rabin. The defense pressed the issue: how could a bullet shot from above travel horizontally from the elbow to the armpit? On March 3, 1996, Dr. Kluger explained that it couldn't.

Dr. Kluger: "You don't have to be a mathematician to understand that a bullet enters a body in a straight line. In order for a shot to enter at 45 degrees, as was the case in the second bullet, the shooter has to be lying down, not standing."

On April 3, 1996 Dr. Yehuda Hiss, the patholgist on duty at Ichilov Hospital, testified just before Rubin was to return to the stand. He said that Dr. Raviv (no apparent relation to Avishai) was the first to examine Rubin and he was apparently not overly concerned.

Dr. Hiss: "In this case, we are talking about a friction wound, that is to say, the bullet just grazed him. It did not penetrate the skin at all. We are talking about a superficial injury that caused a minor scrape."

So why, according to the newspapers, was Rubin hospitalized for five days? And why, to this day, does the Israeli public think the courageous Rubin took a serious wound in the arm?

Because another doctor, Yoram Hamo reported that: "There was a gunshot wound under the elbow. Under the armpit two entrance wounds were found."

How can two doctors at the same hospital produce two such drastically different reports? Dr. Hiss has Rubin not shot at all, merely grazed, while Dr. Hamo originally concludes he was shot twice. Later, he claimed that the x-rays revealed two exit wounds in the armpit made by one bullet.

Something was very wrong about Rubin's account of how he was shot and he was in trouble when he sat down to testify after Hiss.

Defense: "On the same night, you testified to the police from the hospital."

Rubin: "That's true. I don't say things that aren't true."

Defense: "A gun was given to Damti [at the hospital]. Was it yours?"

Rubin: "Yes. Damti was the departed Prime Minister's driver, bless his memory. I was afraid, I didn't know who was passing in the corridor. I feared that an Arab or some minority member would take my gun and I asked Damti to watch it for me. That's all."

How likely is it that Arabs were roaming around the corridor where the Prime Minister and his bodyguard were being treated? What other minorities was Rubin afraid of? In fact, the corridor was crawling with security personnel. Why did Rubin give his gun to Damti? More to the point, what did Damti need it for at that moment? Rubin's gun was not examined by the police and ceased being an issue at the trial.

Defense: "Before the rally, were you shown photos of suspects?"
Rubin: "I'm not interested in answering that." [The court requested that the witness write his answer on a piece of paper and submit
it to the judges].

Needless to say, as attorney Fleishmann told *Anashim* magazine,
if Rubin agreed to write the answer for the judges, it had to have
been a "Yes." What the court is not told, is that Rubin actually knew
Amir personally. They were aquaintances at Bar Ilan University and
he well knew about Amir's threats on Rabin's Life.

Defense: "Tell us what happened after the first shot."
Rubin: "I grabbed Yitzhak as I previously explained, we began
falling together, and as we were going down but not yet on the
ground, I heard another shot. I identified the third shot while we
were on the ground. I was hit with the second shot."

Rubin completely altered his story to fit the new evidence. Since
medically and ballistically he could not have been shot while lying
down, he adds yet another version of events to his previous testimony to the court, police and Shamgar Commission. Now he was
shot at the exact moment he began to fall. In other words, while
almost standing. And how does he explain his about-turn and the
threat of being charged with perjury?

Rubin: [to the court] "My previous testimony was taken an hour
after the event while I was under tranquilizing medicine and in
pain. If there are things that aren't exact, that could be why."
Defense: "You previously testified... [testimony concerning bullet
read]."
Rubin: "Here, the version is mistaken. The real story is that I was
in a bent position just beginning to fall."

The fact that he was not on tranquilizers at the Shamgar
Commission, or during his first session at the court, or when questioned by the police, and still told a very different account, wasn't
even questioned.

Chapter Fifteen
THE "KILLER" SPEAKS

As far as anyone can tell, Yigal Amir is certain he murdered Yitzhak Rabin. Until, May, 1997, hints to the contrary were mostly withheld from the public. There were two exceptions. At his hearing in December, 1995 Amir asked reporters why they didn't investigate the murder of Rabin's bodyguard (Yoav Kuriel). He continued, "The whole business has been a farce. The entire system is rotten. I will be forgiven when people know the whole story." Then he was taken back to his Shabak cell until his trail; where he returned to his previous smirking, grinning, laughing, incomprehensible demeanor.

Behind closed doors, Amir was different. However, almost nothing revealing said to the authorities was released. A rare exception occurred in January, 1996 when *Maariv* printed a statement to a police investigator from November 21, 1995.

Amir: They're going to kill me in here.
Investigator: Nonsense.
Amir: You don't believe me, well I'm telling you it was a conspiracy. I didn't know I was going to kill Rabin.
Investigator: What do you mean? You pulled the trigger, it's that simple.
Amir: Then why didn't Raviv report me? He knew I was going to do it and he didn't stop me. And why didn't anyone shoot me to save Rabin?

On numerous occasions Amir said he didn't know he was going to kill Rabin. What did he mean by that? By the time the Shamgar Commission began its inquiry, he had a story ready to cover the question. He didn't know he was going to kill Rabin, he explained to the commission, he thought he was only going to paralyze him with a shot to the spine.

But he said much more to the Shamgar Commission that was hidden from the public. In May, 1997, the weekly newspaper *Yerushalayim* published a three part series of Amir's testimony to the Shamgar Commission's investigators Amir Zolty and Sigal Kogot.

Since this was a complete unedited transcript, much of what Amir says is didactic and boring. Nonetheless, he reveals a great deal of important information that he never recounted in open court when it may have helped him.

We begin with an enormously important observation. Previously, this book compared the still photo of Amir from the Kempler film published by *Yediot Ahronot* with Amir's reconstruction of the shooting. The picture shows "Amir" shooting from the wrong hand. If that wasn't proof enough that another person was superimposed over Amir, he provides the coup de grace.

Amir On The Kempler Film:

Shamgar Investigators (SI): In one of the segments you are filmed shoulder to shoulder with three policemen.

Amir: I saw the picture in the newspaper. Very strange.

SI: Do you recall what they said in this segment?

Amir: I want to see that tape, there are some really weird things in it.

SI: What's weird?

Amir: I look weird in it, I don't know.

SI: Really?

Amir: What I'm wearing, the shirt. It's not just that they colored it in, they colored it blue in the papers. That's nonsense. I have to see the tape.

SI: A tricot shirt.

Amir: You see that it was rolled up to here (half way). In the paper you don't see that.

SI: And in the paper you are shooting from the left. But it wasn't that way.

Amir: I shoot from the left hand?

SI: You have to see the tape.

Amir notes that his shirt was rolled up past his elbows, yet in the stills of the Kempler film published in *Yediot Ahronot,* the shooter is wearing a long sleeved shirt. As soon as I read this quote, I rewatched the Kempler film. There was Amir either wearing a short sleeved shirt or as he claims, a long sleeved shirt rolled up. And worse, the Shamgar Commission knew it, but never entered the fact into the public records. Instead the commission curtly and quickly dismissed all evidence of a conspiracy. But it was the commission's investigators who pointed out the fact to Amir that he appeared in the film's still picture shooting with the wrong hand.

And what does Amir mean that his shirt was colored in? In the film he is wearing a distinctly blue shirt. But Amir seems to be saying that his shirt's color was altered or enhanced; However, someone else at the murder scene thought it was blue.

Who Was That Usher?

SI: You spoke of someone in a beret who tried to remove you or something like that. We don't know who he is.

Amir: Yes, he was some kind of usher. I don't exactly know what he was.

SI: You said he wore a tricot shirt with a beret on its side.

Amir: He stood there all the time. He was an older man.

SI: And what is this that suddenly he said, "Tell them to come to you?"

Amir: Just interesting.

SI: Were there barriers up?

Amir: Not yet. They began tearing down barriers. They photographed me from the moment I arrived.

SI: We don't see you arriving. We see you at a later stage on the potted plant.

Amir: The potted plant was at the end, a minute or two before.

SI: We see you five minutes before.

Amir: Yes, that's the potted plant I sat on...

SI: Alright, now you're standing two meters from the scene. People are approaching you and you have to explain your presence. Did you say you were a chauffeur?

Amir: No, because they'd ask to see my license and things could get messy. I thought I'd just act innocent, say I wanted to see Rabin ... I hung around the cops saying nothing. So if they said that everyone had to leave, they would think I belonged there ... Shulamit Aloni* arrived and the usher appeared, causing a small problem.

SI: What did he do? What did he say?

Amir: He said [to unidentified security personnel], "Did you block

---

*   Shulamit Aloni is a leader of the left-wing Meretz Party.

the back of the parking lot?" They answered no. So he announced over his radio that it should be barricaded there.

SI: Who are you talking about, the usher in the beret you just showed us?

Amir: Yes, I think. I thought it was strange that he was a civilian ordering policemen around. But I thought he was an organizer of the demonstration. Then he sent a policeman to clear out the crowd. Another policeman and a driver were ordered to leave.

SI: Did the bodyguard beside Rabin's car see you?

Amir: Yes, but he didn't point me out. He gazed at the crowd.

SI: Were the barriers up?

Amir: There weren't any. There were lots of policemen and no one could get in. After the driver left, the usher came up to me and asked, "Was he one of yours?" meaning the policeman. Then I understood he bought my act.

SI: Did he ask you about the driver?

Amir: I don't know. I don't like to lie so I said, "I don't know him. He was here by the car all the time." The usher made a round and came back to order another driver beside me out. Then a policeman came and escorted him away. He shouted, "No, no. The one in the blue shirt."

SI: To you?

Amir: Don't know but he pointed in an odd way, like this, he pointed a bit at someone. The policeman came back to me and asked, "Where is your car?" I said, "Here, here." He said, "Good," and left. I continued standing in the same spot.

Amir says he was photographed from the moment he arrived. But by whom?

He appears in the Kempler film only for the last five minutes before the shooting. He managed to get into the sterile zone because no barriers were put up. Then an "usher" in civilian clothes cleared out everyone around Amir, including policemen and chauffers but left him in place.

Obviously if this "usher" was clearing out all the other drivers, Amir should have been removed with them. One driver suspected Amir of something and shouted to a policeman that he is the one who should be escorted out. Minutes before the assassination, all unauthorized personnel were removed from the sterile zone except Amir by an "usher" of whom the Shamgar Commission investigators had no knowledge whatsoever.

Amir On Like-Minded Friends

Amir: I got to the demonstration and saw a friend from Likud youth on a bus. He told me that Itamar Ben Gvir wanted to kill Rabin tonight. "You know about this, of course," he said. "I told the police about it." I laughed. In recollection I can't figure this one out. But there were a lot of strange things ... I walked to the stage but security was too tight so I walked towards the parking lot. I saw a friend of mine behind there. A real left-winger from law school. So I walked around and entered from the other side, and just as I arrived, they began removing people from there.

Admittedly, the left-wing friend from school could have been in the murder zone quite by accident. Or, perhaps he was surveilling Amir. But the fact that Itamar Ben Gvir was there is more than merely significant. He was a highly publicized extremist, famous for stalking and harassing Rabin. A month before, the media reported that he left a note on the windshield of Rabin's car: "If I can get to his car, I can get to Rabin." He threatened to kill Rabin that night and the police were informed. Therefore, they should have been on high alert against the possibility of a religious Jew in his 20s shooting Rabin.

But Gvir and Amir were not the only young potential religious assassins. Buried in the police records of the assassination night is the report of police officer Shlomo Eyal who wrote, "During the rally I spotted two young men in *kipas* carrying bags who looked out of place. With the help of a uniformed policeman, I checked the bags and examined their IDs. One was named Noam Freidman. We let them go." The other out-of-place young man was not named.

Noam Freidman was a future political murderer. In March, 1997, it looked like Prime Minister Netanyahu was not going to convince his cabinet to support an Israeli withdrawal from Hebron. The cabinet was evenly divided on the issue and its fate lay with three fence sitters.

Then a soldier arrived in Hebron and started shooting up the marketplace in front of cameras from three international networks. He was apprehended after killing one Arab and wounding six. The

Arabs were about to riot when the PLO's intelligence chief Jibril Rajoub arrived from Jericho twenty minutes later. After he calmed the situation down, all three wavering cabinet ministers chose to support withdrawal.

By the next day, it was obvious to many that there was much wrong with the scenario. Freidman was expelled from his yeshiva a year before for "unstable behaviour," and was admitted to a government psychiatric hospital for six months. He was released and shortly after, decided to join the army. The recruiting center was warned in a letter from the city of Maaleh Adumim's Social Welfare Department (Friedman's hometown) not to accept Freidman nor ever "place him in any position requiring a weapon." Yet despite his long stay in the hospital, his disturbing school record and a municipal warning, Freidman was drafted. After his shooting spree, the IDF promised a full explanation of his inexplicable recruitment. It was never released.

Suspicions arose that the IDF deliberately recruited unstable young men for devious purposes. These suspicions were reinforced by the impossible appearance of Jibril Rajoub in Hebron. At the time, the city was in Israeli hands and Rajoub had no right to be in it without prior permission. He explained to the newspaper *Kol Ha'ir* that he heard about the shooting over the radio and immediately travelled to Hebron at 180 km/hr. However, even at this breakneck illegal speed, he could not have made the 90 minute trip in twenty minutes. In short, the Freidman shooting, like Amir's, also looked like a staged incident.

So what was this killer doing that night at Kings of Israel Square? As researcher Yechiel Mann observes, "He wasn't there to celebrate peace or to hear Aviv Gefen."

Amir On Arabs

Avishai Raviv's superiors, Officers Kheshin and Barak testified to the Shamgar Commission that he reported only on Amir's violent intentions towards Arabs and not on his violent intention towards Rabin. Amir, they insisted, was a potential threat to Arabs. He tells a different story.

SI: Did you organize against Arabs?

Amir: No, no. This is nonsense from the media.

SI: This wasn't the media, rather what others said in their investigations.

Amir: I said we have to protect settlements. But hurt Arabs? In wartime, yes but never kill them before, God forbid ... I'm alright with the enemy.

Amir On Eyal

Yigal Amir was supposed to have been an active member of the extremist group, Eyal.

SI: Did Kach or Eyal members come to your seminars?

Amir: They came just one sabbath but I threw them out. I really gave it to them. I can't stand their types, just don't publicize that fact.

SI: There were youths who came to Hebron on the Sabbath and overturned market stalls.

Amir: Not with my group, never. Ask anyone. I didn't let anyone near them. Once, at Orient House some of them tried causing chaos but I gave it to them but good because I can't stand that kind of nonsense ... I wasn't familiar with extremist groups ... Don't believe me, but I'm not a radical.

While Amir's claim of not harming Arabs is borne out by ample testimony, his non-association with radical groups, especially Eyal, does not correspond with the facts. He may have been trying to protect people from arrest by association with him. Then again, consider his testimony regarding Avishai Raviv.

Amir On Raviv:

Amir: I became acquainted with Avishai Raviv at university. He was nothing on campus. He would organize sabbath events and people didn't come. I came because it was important for me to see the places. I didn't admire him for his organizing talents ... He was on the fringes before he met me. Only through my seminars did he gain legitimacy. I didn't understand why he would destroy it all the time with his publicized swearing-in ceremonies and the like. Now I understand a lot of things, many more things ... After the Goldstein [massacre], Raviv moved to Kiryat Arba and everyone told me he worked for the Shabak. Despite the rising suspicions, I got to know him as a person and I was a bit opposed to it all ... After Goldstein, there were a lot of arrests and people suspected Raviv was behind them. So they told me not to befriend him. I answered that even if he is a Shabak agent, he's a human being ... Avishai Raviv helped me a lot. He brought me a cellphone, he brought me lots of things ... I have friends who are spiritual pals, who I can talk to and Avishai was a friend like that. He's immature and does a lot of stupid things but he's a good guy and I appreciate his character. There are very positive sides to it. He would arrange visits to childrens' hospitals and old folks homes just to make everybody happy. I still believe in him. I know he has a good heart.

SI: There were witnesses who saw you and Raviv discussing murdering Rabin with a group of Kahanists.

Amir: It's true that Avishai Raviv also said that Rabin needed to be murdered but I wasn't sitting with this group.

SI: Did you ever hear Avishai Raviv say that Rabin needed to be killed?

Amir: Yes, I heard that lots of times.

According to Amir, Raviv was a hapless organizer, on the fringes of university life until he came along and legitimized him. And all the while he was boosting Raviv's career, he knew he was a Shabak agent. Even so, he didn't mind Raviv supplying him with a cellphone and other goods because Raviv was basically good-hearted. Good-hearted even though he constantly expressed his view that Rabin had to be murdered.

What we have here is one inconsistent story. If Amir knew Raviv was a Shabak agent, he should have had nothing to do with him ... unless he had his own Shabak ties.

Amir On The Shabak

Amir: In the past year I had exact information about Rabin's movements. I knew which rally he would appear at, where he was going, every place he went. They pressed the Shabak into service against the people. And what are they doing after the assassination? Repressing the people more. It's absurd. It wasn't their incitement that caused me to do what I did ... The head of Shabak said a lone gunman would never murder Rabin. So he incited lone gunmen to try.

SI: Where did you hear he said that?

Amir: It was around. People think Rabin was killed because the Shabak didn't interfere with the murder. I say they couldn't have stopped it.

He takes the same attitude with the previous intelligence agency he worked directly for.

Amir On Riga, Latvia.

SI: We want to hear about your emissarial work in the Soviet Union in 1992. There are a thousand and one speculations about this period. What did you do there?

Amir: The Liaison Office isn't so secret anymore. Once it was secret. They wanted organizers for Zionist activities and Hebrew teachers, all kinds of things. They asked my army unit (the religious Yeshivat Hesder) to send people. Every two months, they would change staff and I went with my friend Avinoam Ezer. When we got there, they were working with 15-year-olds, trying to convince them to immigrate. I thought this was all wrong, that it was smarter to target older students. So I went out in the street with a kipah on my head and found them. I was a real attraction, a Yemenite with a *kipah* and eventually gathered 100 students around me for social events. It was a huge success ...

As far as anyone recalls, Amir was a shy, introverted boy in high school yeshiva and far from a gregarious soldier. However, his personality changed drastically in Riga. It is most unlikely that on his own initiative he went out on the streets collecting students. Nativ was an intelligence branch, not a free school. Amir was given practical training in social organization and returned to Israel with a new character and perhaps a mission he didn't understand.

SI: Were there bodyguards there?

Amir: Now you're jumping ahead.

SI: We understand you went through a personal security course.

Amir: Nothing, not a thing. Just minor security training. What are you implying? We didn't have weaponry, just tear gas.

Nativ members are not known for their openness. Even after over forty years of existence, little is known of its operations. Amir, almost certainly was on some kind of intelligence mission in Riga, however minor. Back in Israel, he duplicated his successes in Latvia on the campus of Bar Ilan University. He became an attraction in Israel even before the murder.

Yigal Amir On The Shooting That Continues to Confuse Him

SI: Try and recall exactly who said "They're blanks," or what was said. Everyone says they heard something different. And try to recall if you said something.

Amir: I didn't say a word. And I wouldn't have said anything because it might have warned them. It's absurd that I would have said anything.

SI: Maybe immediately after to save yourself, for example?

Amir: No. The "blanks" shout happened before I was pushed to the ground. It was during the shooting. It's difficult for a person to shoot and shout, you're concentrating so much.

SI: In the army they shout, "Fire, fire," while shooting.

Amir: Only in dry runs. I didn't shout anything. I distinctly remember that someone on my right shouted it.

SI: What were his exact words?

Amir: "It's a blank, it's not real." I'm not sure of the exact words but that was the message.

SI: Not something like, "Cease fire?"

Amir: No, no. It was, "It's a blank, it's not real."

SI: How did the shots sound to you?

Amir: I'm not positive. I remember I shot, they pounced on me and I got off two more shots. I recall the first thing the police asked me on the ground was if I had shot a blank or not. I didn't answer but then I remembered someone shouting "blank" while I was shooting. It stuck in my mind; "What is he trying to do to, screw up my mind?" I don't know, it was very weird. It didn't make sense that a bodyguard at the moment they're shooting at his Prime Minister would ask if it was a blank. He would first count on the worst case. Unless he was expecting something else.

SI: None of the bodyguards said it was him.

Amir: Does it appear likely to you that he would admit it today? They'd finish him off.

Amir does know more than he is telling, probably a great deal more. But he is either too frightened, too disturbed or ignorant to say anything resembling the the whole truth.

There was no reason for the Shabak to keep Amir locked up in solitary confinement for a month after the murder. He had already cooperated with the police and confessed. He should have seen his lawyer and family within days. But it was a month before the Shabak felt he was ready to speak to civilians. One can easily imagine the kinds of gruesome pressure applied on him to stick to one self-incriminating story.

But the investigators refused to give up. They wanted to solve the central mystery of the "blanks" shout and ideally, they wanted Amir to confess to the shouting. The questioning continued during the next session.

SI: You know we have witnesses who say you did the shouting.

Amir: I've heard that, but it's not true. It was someone to my right, one of the bodyguards. I'm not sure if it was the one in the black suit or the other one, but it was one of them. I was shocked. Instead of acting to help him, they shouted that the bullets were blanks. There are very strange things going on there.

SI: What strange things?

Amir: While I'm shooting, he shouts, "They're blanks." I don't remember if I heard it after the first shot or the second or third.

SI: Some say it was the police who shouted it.

Amir: Not the police. No, no. It was a bodyguard. When I heard the shout, I was shocked. What, didn't I check the bullets? A bodyguard when he hears a shot, he doesn't stop to ask if they're blanks. He may as well just go home for a nap if he does that. He has to take action.

The Shabak is trained to shoot an assassin in 0.8 seconds. It takes longer to shout, "They're blanks. They're not real." Had the bodyguards shot instead of shouted, Amir could not have fired the alleged two more rounds. He realizes that something is terribly wrong, but stops well short of saying that perhaps, he did shoot a blank just like the bodyguard(s) said.

Amir: I aimed at his spinal cord, not at his heart, his spine ... I wanted to paralyse him, not kill him. After the shot, I stopped shooting to see what kind of reaction, bodily reaction there was.

SI: Was there any reaction?

Amir: Nothing, he continued standing in the same way. Then they jumped on me from the sides and I shot twice more. But I don't remember anything about those shots. I never even saw Rabin's back.

Amir aimed for the spine and shot Rabin in the back. But to his surprise, Rabin didn't even flinch. So he fired again while being pounced on from all sides. But he didn't see his quarry, couldn't take aim, and doesn't know if he actually hit anyone.

Perhaps now he might understand why they shouted, "It's a blank. It's not real."

Chapter Sixteen
THE RIOT BACKFIRES—WITNESSES EMERGE

On April 3, 1997, I was scheduled to speak at Hebrew University for a lecture organized by the Association of Foreign Students, an official students organization belonging to the campus student council. However two left-wing student groups, Meretz and the Labor Party-affiliated Ofek decided to sabotage the engagement. Over several days prior to the lecture they tore down advertising posters and leaked disinformation to the media. It was announced that I was a member of organized crime, didn't live in Israel, was sponsored by radical organizations, and that I was a Holocaust denier. This final accusation was especially insulting; for a full third of my family had been wiped out in the Holocaust.

When the night of the lecture arrived, the saboteurs were ready. The rioters in purple Meretz t-shirts blocked my way, but allowed enough room for an obscure Labor Party Knesset Member, Eitan Cabel, to attack me in front of the cameras with shouts of, "Fascist, fascist, don't hit me," trying to provoke me into throwing a punch. He managed only to look like a fool. Just as I managed to slip inside the lecture hall, the riot began in earnest.

About 150 people came to see me. Their entrance was violently blocked by about five of the 50 protesters who were there. The two "student" leaders were in their early 30s. They appeared to scuffle with student security men, but as the organizer of the lecture, Brian Bunn, later informed me, "Most of the security men wore Meretz shirts under their uniforms. They were there to promote the riot not prevent it."

Had the police arrived before a plate glass window was smashed and people, including one 75-year-old woman, were beaten, the staged riot could have been immediately quashed by simply arresting the two instigators. However, two campus security officers later informed me that the president of the university had issued orders long before not to allow the audience into the lecture hall. And according to numerous people who called the police, the university refused to allow their squad cars to enter the campus grounds.

Journalists, however, were permitted entrance, supposedly to record my humiliation. Undaunted, I presented evidence and logically explained what I would have said, had I been allowed to continue. A few of the reporters started listening. Two campus cops tried to remove me and escort me to a private meeting with the same Knesset member who had just attacked me. I stood my ground, and the reporters took notes.

As expected, most of them wrote the usual disinformation. And yet a few, including the usually benign *Jerusalem Post,* published balanced reports. Others still, including *Yerushalayim* and *Vesti,* published lengthy, favorable articles. Undoubtedly to the dismay of those who planned this riot to shut me up, even my television appearances were dignified. The result was a significant victory for truth.

The most profound result of the national publicity which erupted around me was that several witnesses came forward with important information. Though fear kept many in the shadows, their words have so far proven tenable.

Prior to the riots, I was interviewed on radio. A listener called the station announcer and asked him to act as an intermediary with me on behalf of his friend. The friend had helped construct the stage for the rally where Rabin was assassinated. The crew constructed the stand with the usual security requirements. Shabak agents ordered the crew to dismantle metal detectors placed to secure the backstage area. In short, he said, Amir or any other armed intruder, was allowed to enter the backstage area undetected.

After the riots, I was contacted by a caller from the north of the country, concerned Yoram Rubin, Rabin's personal bodyguard.

"I think this is very important," said the caller. "I know Yoram Rubin's family well. I've known Yoram since he was a baby in Acco. The family has a history that should have prevented Yoram from even joining the Shabak, let alone becoming the Prime Minister's closest bodyguard.

"The father ruled his sons like a Gestapo chieftain. He worked for the government in an intelligence capacity and was very secretive about everything, especially his work. The sons grew up under his abnormal discipline. One son, Gershon, cracked after the family moved to Karmiel twenty years ago. He got badly hooked on hard drugs and stabbed his girlfriend "11" times. He got a life sentence for murder and died in prison, supposedly a suicide.

"So how does a guy like that become the Shabak's choice of guard for Rabin? Do you know the kind of psychological and background tests they do before they'll induct you? I do. Yoram would never have passed. Something is really wrong here."

S., who lives on a moshav, had a scare when he noticed something in the newspapers. He had saved the papers of early November, 1995, as did many people for historical reasons. Included in the newspapers were the photos of Amir reconstructing the assassination. Just over a month later, the Kempler video of the murder was announced. The papers printed half-page photo stills taken from the video of Amir at the moment of shooting.

S. compared the photos of Amir reconstructing the assassination, on the 16th of November, just two weeks after it occurred. He was astounded. While reconstructing the murder, Amir shot the weapon with his right hand. Not surprising since he is right-handed. But, in the Kempler film stills, "Amir" shoots with his left hand extended. And there is absolutely no mistaking it.

Deeply disturbed, he took the photos to two Jerusalem newspapers. They confirmed his suspicions and more. The possibility of one photo being a reversed negative was eliminated. A reverse view would not alter the position of the shooting arm, it would still be left handed. Further, the profile of Amir without long, scruffy sideburns does not resemble Amir's side view in other photos taken the same day.

The newspaper editors would not publish the photos and warned him about showing them to anyone else. This was followed by threatening anonymous phone calls to his home.

The information proved accurate. I discovered the stills were tampered with in other ways and that the Shamgar Commission knew about it. The evidence cannot be hidden nor can its conclusion; someone else's picture was superimposed over that of Amir.

Yoav Kuriel was the suspected Shabak agent who died not long after Rabin. After the cause of death was ruled suicide, his vital organs were removed and he was buried in a closed casket.* Traffic at Hayarkon Junction was detoured for 90 minutes while the funeral took place. This inexplicable honor for an unknown suicide victim led to numerous reporters trying to connect his death to the Rabin assassination. None succeeded, but I was informed tersely and succinctly that Yoav Kuriel didn't commit suicide.

Kuriel's hospital death certificate, in an illegal exception does not list the cause of death. And in an apparent contradiction to the grandeur of the funeral itself, *Maariv* reporter David Ronen found his grave in a lonely corner of Hayarkon cemetary. His name is almost impossible to read. It is nearly an unmarked grave, hardly a hallmark of Jewish tradition.

An informant told me, "I saw Yoav Kuriel's body. I wasn't the only one. It had six or seven bulletholes in the chest. That's not how people commit suicide." He told me we might meet in the future. But he never called back.

Not a week later, Ronnie Schwartz called me from Kfar Saba. He told me a friend of the gravedigger who buried Kuriel told him that Kuriel had seven bullet holes in his chest. Others were also told this information by the gravedigger, but he himself chose to remain out of sight.

The gravedigger, I was told, "Is not a Zionist and he won't risk his life for the country. He saw what happens if you get the wrong people angry."

On May 17, I was given Yoav Kuriel's social security file. I called

---

* Jewish Israelis are usually buried in simple sheets.

Ronen and he came to my home to examine it. "There it is," he said after a quick perusal. "He was employed by the Israel Police at Sheikh Jarrah Headquarters. That's where the police intelligence branch is located."

Kuriel's was not the only suspicious "suicide" connected to the assassination. An American student at Bar Ilan University, David Newman, also supposedly killed himself because he was "depressed" about Rabin's death. A friend of his informed me, "He was close with Avishai Raviv. The night of the assassination, Raviv phoned him and tried to get Newman to implicate himself in the murder. None of his friends bought the suicide story. He was shut up permanently."

Professor Arieh Rosen-Tzvi was the Tel Aviv University law professor who was a member of the Shamgar Commission. He died of cancer not long after the commission's findings were released. I received a phone call from someone who knew him. The caller said he had important information but he could not repeat it over the phone. The next day we met at my home.

The informant holds a most respected position in the educational field. He said, "I saw Arieh the week he died. He told me he was keeping deep secrets in his heart about Rabin and could never reveal them. A few days later he was dead. Cancer isn't a heart attack. You are bedridden in the final stages. He couldn't have died overnight from it."

The story was eerily reminiscent of another death connected to Rabin. At 8:45 on a warm, July morning in 1995, Rabin's deputy defense minister Motta Gur was found dead in his home. He had shot himself through the neck and had supposedly left a one line note saying he didn't want his family to suffer from his pain anymore. The note was never shown publicly. By 5:00 that evening, in unseemly haste, General Gur, the liberator of Jerusalem and a national hero was buried. The reason given by the media for the suicide was Gur's depression over his terminal cancer.

Just a few weeks before, Gur caused an uproar in the Knesset when, according to *Maariv,* June 15, 1995, "It's not that Gur did not merely condemn the settlers, he came to their defense. 'I must say I asked myself why we didn't settle the place years ago? In 1946, as youths, we founded thirteen kibbutzim the same way.' Gur's pronouncement led to hours of vigorous debate which almost resulted in several MKs [Members of the Knesset] being ejected from the forum."

Gur was actively opposing Rabin's "peace" process. He had recently visited Hebron and the nearby settlement of Barkai to encourage the settler movement. The settlers, in return, considered him their only friend left in Rabin's cabinet. And as Rabin's deputy in the Defense Ministry, he was privy to the kind of secrets those opposed to the "peace" process might find most useful.

But, terminal cancer led to Gur taking his own life. Or did it? Not according to Gur's physician and the head of Ichilov Hospital's Oncology Department where he was being treated, Prof. Samario Chaitchik who told *Maariv*, "Two months ago we found a brain tumor. It was treated at Memorial Hospital in Manhattan. Seven weeks ago, Gur returned to Israel. He was greatly improved and his tumor completely disappeared, as did the side effects of his treatment. We saw him three days ago and he showed no signs of depression. He made an appointment to see us in ten days."

The night before his death he made another appointment, this time to be interviewed by television reporter Avi Bettleheim. Family and friends all expressed utter surprise at the death. Gur was not the suicidal kind.

And he, a cabinet member, was buried within eight hours of this death, long before a proper funeral could be arranged.

Gur's suspicious death was just five months before his boss, Yitzhak Rabin was assassinated.

Chapter Seventeen
ANOTHER RESEARCHER, AT LAST

In October, 1996, television Channel Two broadcast a report about people who deny the official version of the Rabin assassination. Though the program was mostly devoted to my research, a few seconds were also given to a researcher from Ramat Gan, Natan Gefen. After seeing the program, a local reporter visited Gefen. In early November, the Ramat Gan newspaper *Hamekomon* published a courageous interview with Gefen, who had been researching the cover-up of the Rabin murder for the past year. According to the article, "Gefen sat in most of the court discussions connected to the murder, met with numerous experts and is certain Yigal Amir had a partner in the murder...who is walking free." After a year of lonely investigation, I discovered, to my great delight, that I was not alone.

What follows are selections from the three page interview. I add that Gefen disagrees with my conclusion that Yigal Amir shot one blank bullet and that Rabin was actually murdered in his car on the way to Ichilov Hospital. However, we were in agreement about details of the Shabak cover-up, which I will comment on at the conclusion of his interview.

Ramat Gan Hamekoman (RGH): Natan Gefen, what is your thesis based on?

Gefen: It's based on an accumulation of facts I read, collected and researched. Yigal Amir claimed in his first interrogation that he hadn't intended to kill Rabin, just wound him. Yet he shot hollowpoint bullets which do much more bodily harm than regular bullets. So he must have been lying. However, hollowpoint bullets have much less penetrating power and he must have been given advance information that Rabin wouldn't be wearing a bulletproof vest. My conclusion is that he had inside information. Also, hollowpoint bullets shatter and cannot be identified once they enter the body.

RGH: These aren't serious claims. Yigal Amir was caught, he shot three times and even reconstructed the event.

Gefen: Yigal Amir shot just once and then was pounced on by Rabin's bodyguards. The next shot was point blank at Rabin and Amir never got that close. Amir never touched Rabin physically.

RGH: How do you know that?

Gefen: From the film of the assassination and according to testimony given by police and Shabak officers.

RGH: Yet, in his reconstruction, Amir shot three times.

Gefen: His reconstruction wasn't accurate. He claimed that after he was held down by the security men, he got off two more shots. I don't believe him. After his gun was taken, the police and Shabak found eight bullets within. Amir claimed he loaded nine. Amir is hiding the facts.

RGH: Let's say you're right, then who shot the other bullets?

Gefen: The answer was smothered previously. I insist that Rabin's bodyguards had to have been arrested on the spot. We're talking about the murder of a Prime Minister, not a break-in. The moment they weren't arrested, they could coordinate their testimony and leave the killer's identity in the hands of the Shabak.

RGH: So you claim that someone from the Shabak shot Rabin?

Gefen: Perhaps, or someone connected to the Shabak, or maybe not.

RGH: In short, you are claiming there was a Shabak conspiracy?

Gefen: No. This was a conspiracy between Amir and a Shabak agent who succeeded in gaining the trust of Rabin's bodyguards who aided in the murder. In my opinion, someone took advantage of the pile-up on Amir to shoot Rabin.

RGH: And who shot the bodyguard Yoram Rubin?

Gefen: I think it was staged because a third bullet was never found. The police criminal investigations laboratory found that the chemical composition of [Rubin's] bullethole was different from the rest of Amir's bullets.

RGH: Amir was interrogated so often, yet you say none of the interrogaters succeeded in getting him to identify his partner in crime?

Gefen: I claim the Shabak ordered him not to reveal anything because the damage it would cause would be greater.

RGH: What interest did Amir have in agreeing?

Gefen: Perhaps they promised him an early release. Amir cooperated fully with the police, confessed and should have been permitted to see an attorney or visitors after a week. But Amir was held for over a month without seeing an outsider. Why? In my opinion, the time was needed to persuade him not to expose a partner connected to the Shabak.

RGH: When did you come to the conclusion that Amir had a partner?

Gefen: Right at the beginning of the events. After the murder, the Shabak acted most peculiarly. Usually, people under investigation try to hide their involvement. That's how the Shabak acted after the Bus 300 incident and the IDF during the Agranat Commission. The speed with which the Shabak took responsibility upon itself and initiated its own inquiry indicates they wanted to short-circuit an even bigger scandal. At the Shamgar Commission, the Shabak tried to prove that they screwed up and that's unnatural. I felt there was something very wrong and I appealed to the State Comptroller and Attorney General to reopen the whole investigation. Neither answered me.

RGH: It seems more than a coincidence that your work appeared on television on the anniversary of the murder.

Gefen: I sought out the media because I knew someone could rub me out. So I sent faxes and letters to as many people as I could so I'd become too known to kill.

RGH: Don't you think your work hurts too many people?

Gefen: And the fact that because of Shabak pressure on Amir, a murderer is loose doesn't? I want to explode the whole matter. There's no telling what the murderer could do if he isn't caught. And if he isn't caught, it is an invitation for the security services to try something again.

I concluded that Gefen had not seen the film of Rabin's back car door closing before he entered the vehicle. If he had, I'm sure he would have concluded that Rabin was shot in the car and not during the confusion of Amir's apprehension. We did agree that someone else shot Rabin and that the Rubin shooting was a red herring. However, based on the same assassination film that clearly shows Rabin unhurt after Amir's shot, I maintained that Amir shot a blank bullet. And though he intended to shoot Rabin, and that makes him guilty of attempted murder, the real dirty work was carried out by someone else.

Those details aside, Gefen's research appeared serious and there was no doubting his bravery or ethical convictions. He deserved the appreciation of all honest Israelis.

Though we disagreed on certain specifics of the conspiracy, Gefen did reveal to me a most chilling piece of evidence:

The initial surgeon's report on Rabin from Ichilov Hospital. In it, he reported that Rabin was shot in the chest from the front, by a bullet which finally shattered his spine.

This was indeed a smoking gun. Gefen's discovery and diligence were most impressive. When the editor and a reporter from the Russian-language newspaper *Vesti* interviewed me after the Hebrew University staged riot, I recommended that they meet with Gefen. The following is Gefen's interview for the piece, published in May, 1997.

Vesti: When did you begin your investigation of the Rabin murder?

Gefen: On the very night of the assassination. I thought it was incredible that the murderer had such an easy time of it. I couldn't understand why Rabin's bodyguards let him down, so as a first step, I decided to record the television coverage of the assassination night. Other questions quickly followed.

Vesti: Such as?

Gefen: Why did Rabin's wife arrive so late at the hospital? Why wasn't the hospital prepared for Rabin in light of the fact that his car had a mobile radio in it? Where was Rabin's car for so long if it only takes two minutes to drive to Ichilov?

Vesti: The Shamgar Commission found no wrongdoing, just negligence, by the bodyguards and the lawyers allowed to see the secret sections of its findings say they reveal nothing but security procedures.

Gefen: Let me ask you a question. Why was the first investigation of the assassination undertaken by Shabak officials? They shouldn't have been investigating, they should have been investigated. And why didn't anybody charged with getting to the truth at least investigate the issue of whether Amir acted alone or not and if not, who was behind him? My duty is to ask questions, not necessarily to answer them. Do you have any answers?

Vesti: No. Do you? What are your conclusions?

Gefen: Yigal Amir didn't act alone. The fatal shot came from a second person and it was through the chest, while Amir shot at the back. The real murderer is walking free. The judges at Amir's trial concluded that Rabin was shot twice. I say he was shot three times, the fatal shot coming from the front. On the night of the murder, Health Minister Ephraim Sneh and Ichilov Hospital's director Gabi Barabash both announced that Rabin was shot in the chest from the front and that he suffered a spinal injury. Both men are doctors who were in the operating room and saw Rabin's body. It's not possible they were mistaken.

Vesti: Where is the bullet that shot Yoram Rubin?

Gefen: I am convinced Rubin's wound was staged. The bullet was never found and the police materials expert, Baruch Gladstein, testified that the bullet which made the hole in his clothing was of a different metallic composition than was found in Amir's other bullets.

He also concluded that one bullet which passed through Rabin's clothing was shot point blank. If you look at the Kempler film, you see that Amir had no possibility of shooting point blank.

Vesti: The film is of such poor quality that you can barely make out details.

Gefen: Come, let's look at the film. I'll show you, in slow motion, how it was doctored. Pay attention to Rabin's reaction after being shot. There are 24 frames per second and if you count frames you can accurately time events. Notice Rabin is shot and then turns his head toward the gunshot. Do you know how long it takes the average healthy person to physically react to shock or pain? 3/4 of a second or 18 frames. And Rabin was no James Bond, he was 72 and in terrible shape. How long did it take Rabin to react? Count the frames, 0.2 seconds. More than half a second was chopped from this part of the film. Now examine the surgeon's report. It reports that Rabin was shot through the chest and spine. Dr. Barabash reports on television soon after that Rabin was given eight units of blood. That means he was bleeding profusely. So where was it? No blood was found on the pavement where he was supposedly shot."

Gefen understated his case. When I later read the full surgeon's report, I discovered that, according to Dr. Gutman, Rabin was given 21 units of blood. He was, thus, bleeding far more profusely than Gefen imagined at the time.

Vesti: I don't see anything strange about that. The onset of bleeding can be delayed. The bleeding must have been profuse after he was put in the car.

Gefen: Not so. When a person is shot fatally, he is lain on the ground and covered with a blanket to prevent more blood loss. There was no way there would be no blood on the pavement. None showed up in the car.

That is, for all we know. Rabin's car was apparently not examined after the assassination. Not once in the Shamgar findings or the transcripts of the Amir trial is there mention of an examination of the car, or its back seat.

Vesti: Who gave you the surgeon's report?

Gefen: Last November the local Ramat Gan newspaper did a story about my research. I copied the article and distributed it throughout Ichilov Hospital. The strategy paid off. Someone faxed me the report anonymously. Immediately after, I sent a copy to the State Comptroller's Office and requested that it reopen an investigation into the Rabin murder. They replied that there already was an official investigation and it would be pointless to open another one.

Vesti: Why is Amir keeping quiet? Doesn't he know someone else shot Rabin?

Gefen: He must know. Amir was arrested and not permitted visitors for a month. Why, if he was cooperating with investigators? Noam Freidman, who shot seven people in Hebron, cooperated and was allowed to see a lawyer the next day. It took the Shabak a month to persuade Amir to cooperate. And did he ever, after that! I sat in most of the sessions of his trial and everytime his lawyers made a strong point in his defense, it was he who cut them off, shouting, "I killed him. I did it by myself." It was obvious overplay by Amir. But it doesn't matter what he says. I have documents that disprove him and they are strong enough to warrant opening a new investigation of the assassination. But the government will never let that happen.

Chapter Eighteen
THE GUN

Immediately after the shooting, a witness, Noam Kedem, told Reuters, "I heard like four, five shots then I saw Rabin collapse." He was one of several witnesses, including policeman Yossi Smadja, who heard five shots. Rabin, according to this account, didn't collapse until after the fourth or fifth shot. Reinterviewed by *Hatikshoret Magazine* in May, 1997, Kedem added another vignette; "I saw a gun clip on the ground. I kicked it towards all the bodyguards." It's possible that amidst all the hubbub, a policeman or bodyguard lost a clip. But there's another possibility. *Maariv* reporter Boaz Gaon, who phoned me after reading the *Hatikshoret* piece, reacted: "It's a strange story. It sounds like there could have been a second gun involved."

This is the thesis of researcher Natan Gefen and a theory presented to the court at Amir's trial by his attorney Gabi Shahar. In short, Amir shot his blank and the real murderer took advantage of the chaos to shoot Rabin.

The thesis is contradicted by the disturbing account of Yevgeny Furman, an outpatient at Ichilov Hospital who told a Reuters' reporter that he saw Rabin in the emergency room: "His eyes were closed and he was bleeding from the back and chest." If there was a frontal chest wound, Amir didn't cause it because he did not shoot from the front. On the other hand, because the chest wound left no bullethole in Rabin's clothing, it couldn't have occurred in the chaos of the Kings of Israel Square parking lot.

Furman's testimony combined with that of Drs. Barabash, Gutman, Sneh and the unnamed pathologist, revealed in a deposition to the Supreme Court that Rabin was shot three times. This is powerful proof that a second gun killed Rabin. But if so, how do we explain the fact that the two bullets pulled out of Rabin's body matched Amir's gun in ballistics tests?

We look for the answer first in the Israel Police Ballistics Laboratory report prepared by ballistics expert Bernard Shechter. He was given a veritable arsenal of ammunition and weaponry to test beginning with Amir's gun. He complained that he should have been given the gun with a bullet still in the chamber, as is standard procedure. He reported that Amir's gun contained eight bullets. "Four were regular bullets, four were Silver-Tip hollowpoints."

Rabin was supposedly killed by two hollowpoints and Rubin shot by a regular bullet. According to the conclusions of the Shamgar Commission, first Amir shot a hollowpoint at Rabin, a regular bullet at Rubin and another hollowpoint at Rabin. At Amir's trial Shechter testified that, "The first two bullets loaded were hollowpoints, followed by a regular bullet." Amir objected to Shechter's tests, insisting that he got the order wrong.

Silver-Tip hollowpoints are often manufactured with a small metal pellet in the tip, which significantly increases damage to the body. Amir testified that he used the most powerful bullets he had available, so two should have been found in Rabin's body. Consider Bernard Shechter's testimony at the Amir trial on March 3, 1996.

Defense: You reported that there were no pellets. Where did you request examination for the pellets?

Shechter: In the x-rays. I asked that they be examined to find the pellets in the body. I don't recall precisely when I made the request but I asked five times after I saw the ammunition and saw the pellet in four other bullets. So, I requested that the pathologist Dr. Hiss please check the x-ray and perhaps find the pellet. He said he checked and checked and didn't find it.

The next day, Dr. Hiss testified about the missing pellets, "Other than the two bullets I removed from the body of the deceased, there were no other foreign particles." Thus, Amir did not use the most damaging bullets at his disposal.

And now the official line becomes downright implausible. Shortly after Amir was arrested, the police raided his parents' home looking for weapons and ammunition. They left empty-handed. Two days later, the Shabak conducted its own search and came up with enough materiel to supply a small militia. It was found in an attic above Yigal's brother Hagai's room. Hagai was accused and later convicted of hollowing out the bullets that killed Rabin. He received a light seven-year sentence based on his testimony that he had no idea his brother intended to murder anyone with the bullets ... as if there is any other good reason for doctoring the ammunition.

Other researchers have been most intrigued by the fact that Shechter found two blank bullets in Hagai's arsenal and a silencer. I am more perplexed by all the rest. Here is a partial list of bullets from Hagai's armory sent to Shechter to test:

- 5 Silver-Tip (hollowpoint) bullets manufactured by Winchester.
- A package of 380 Winchester Automatic Super-X bullets.
- Two bullets found in Rabin's body were Silver-Tip (hollow-points) manufactured by Winchester.

Which brings us to the confusion; if Hagai Amir had hundreds of factory-made hollowpoint bullets in his attic, why would he need to hollow out his brother's bullets? The bullets shot at Rabin were already hollowed out by Winchester. The power of these bullets is commonly enhanced by the addition of a small metal pellet inserted into the tip. These were not found in Rabin's body.

To sidestep these problems, the official version has Hagai Amir further hollowing out manufactured hollowpoints and in doing so, removing the small metal pellet. Now why would he do such a thing? Winchester doesn't need his help to beef up its bullets and by removing the metal pellet, he achieved the opposite effect.

Dr. Hiss only adds to the confusion when, in the same session, he testifies that the second bullet which hit Rabin was shot horizontally. Amir backed him up later when he testified that he never lowered his gun. But the Shamgar Commission concluded that Amir shot Rabin from above the second time while he was prone on the ground. Until Yoram Rubin renounced all of his previous testimony about how he was shot, the state's case was based on the peculiar testimony of police officer Yisrael Gabai for much of the trial.

Defense: Do you recall testifying that you saw the defendant holding his gun at a 45 degree angle?
Gabai: I recall. I don't recall giving a statement to the police to the same effect. I don't know why I didn't tell this to the police.
Defense: How come no other policeman said the same thing about the angle?
Gabai: Ask them.
Defense: How can it be that after three months yours is the only testimony in court recalling the defendant holding the gun at a 45 degree angle?
Gabai: I told what I saw. As for the other policemen, ask them.
Defense: You meant, 45 degrees from the ground.
Gabai: Yes. While he held the gun in that position, no one was on top of him yet. While I was running at him, I saw the defendant standing with the gun pointed at 45 degrees towards the ground. I don't know how many people were beside the Prime Minister, but not one jumped on him [Amir], though they were only a meter's distance from him.
Defense: So you're saying the gun held by the defendant was pointed to the ground?
Gabai: True.

So ends part one of Gabai's testimony. In contradiction to a dozen or so witnesses who saw Amir pounced on immediately after the first shot, Gabai insists no one touched him and he stood alone shooting down on the fallen Rabin and Rubin. If believed, Gabai is the only eyewitness to the murder who saw things this way. But there were more problems with his testimony than solutions, the first and most obvious being, why didn't the bodyguards do their duty vis a vis Amir? So, the court eventually rejected Gabai's testimony and accepted Rubin's newfound version that Amir, in fact, did shoot horizontally.

Now to Act Two of Officer Gabai's illuminating testimony.

Defense: You told the court that you were ordered to look for bullet cartridges?
Gabai: Correct. I found a 9 mm cartridge but the area commander told me to look for .22 cartridges.
Defense: You saw the gun before you went looking for the cartridges.
Gabai: As soon as the defendant was down, the gun was taken by an anti-terror officer. I saw the gun.

He then testified that the gun was taken by a police officer of an anti-terrorist unit. This will be significant shortly.

Defense: But you didn't get a close look at the gun?
Gabai: Before I found the cartridge, I could tell what kind of a gun it was.
Defense: And you couldn't tell what kind of cartridge?
Gabai: I asked the area commander why on earth he told me to look for a .22 cartridge.
Defense: And the cartridge you found was right beside the Prime Minister's car.
Gabai: Correct.
Defense: And it had to be from the gun that shot the Prime Minister?
Gabai: I didn't know then. I found a cartridge and I kept it.
Defense: So why didn't you ask the area commander why you were looking for a .22 if you already found a different gauge?
Gabai: No. No, I didn't see the gun and I didn't know what gauge

it was. I heard three shots and I didn't know if the bodyguards or police shot them. I thought the actual gun the Prime Minister was shot with was a .22 and I understood this from the area commander.

Quite a quick about-turn. Gabai first saw the gun and then he didn't. He first thought the bullets must be 9 mm and then he didn't. Clearly if the area commander ordered him to look for a .22 bullet at that moment, there must have been a good reason. But the defense pursued it and failed to extract it from Gabai. Exasperated, Amir's attorney tried a new line of questioning, but inexplicably failed to properly follow-up.

Defense: Did you ask the area commander if you should also look for a .22 gun?
Gabai: I didn't ask.
Defense: Were you forewarned that there was suspicion of trouble at the rally.
Gabai: Yes, but from Arabs, not of an attack on the Prime Minister from one of the crowd.
Defense: Weren't you informed of potential suspects in the crowd?
Gabai: No.

Quite a police force. Amir was told at the rally by a member of Likud youth that word was out that Itamar Ben Gvir, a well-publicized enemy of Rabin, had vowed to kill him that evening. The Likud youth told Amir that he had already reported the threat to the police. So why wasn't this death threat from a serious and dangerous enemy of Rabin's taken seriously by the police? Why wasn't Gabai, and presumably all other officers, forewarned to look for a potential assassin from the crowd and to apprehend Ben Gvir on the spot?

Amir's attorney attempted to draw the answer out of police officer Yoav Gazit and received a remarkable piece of testimony.

Defense: When you interrogated the defendant on March 12, the name Itamar Ben Gvir came up.
Gabai: We know who he is. He has no connection to the incident.

Yigal connected him to the incident but later recanted. He gave all kinds of theories to the Shabak ... He said that Avishai Raviv passed on blank bullets to Itamar Ben Gvir and that it was done in coordination with the Shabak...

Defense: We have a report that the Shabak was responsible for the [police] investigation. Do you know why?

Gabai: No idea but the Shabak was the dominant factor at certain points in the investigation.

Defense: Why did the Shabak receive responsibility for the investigation?

Gabai: I'm not authorized to tell you...

Defense: How did you feel about the Shabak's role?

Gabai: I didn't appreciate it.

Amir, in fact, almost never theorized in all his testimony. His statement that Avishai Raviv passed blank bullets to Ben Gvir under instructions from the Shabak is an extremely rare glimpse into what secrets Amir may be holding onto. It is the first and only time that he connects Raviv, the Shabak, a potential assassin and blank bullets together. Amir, however momentarily, believed that a second "assassin" already reported to the police, was at the rally carrying a gun loaded with blanks supplied by Avishai Raviv. Were these the .22 cartridges Gazit was told to look for?

The court did not allow exploration of such "side" issues as the area commander's orders to find .22 cartridges because Bernard Shechter testified that the bullets pulled out of Rabin's body by the pathologist Dr. Hiss ballistically matched Amir's gun. The problem with this assumption is that Hiss had no idea what happened to the bullets after he put them in a safe. He admitted to the court, "A policeman took the bullets I removed from Rabin and transferred them to the police laboratory the next day. I don't know his name and I don't recall what he looked like, but they were transferred."

But Yoram Rubin, Rabin's bodyguard, testified that, "The bullets and clothes were taken by Yuval Schwartz, a friend of mine from work." In other words, Rubin said the bullets were taken by a Shabak agent. So which was it, the policeman without a face according to Dr. Hiss or a Shabak agent, according to Rubin?

In fact, there are no records that clearly explain how the bullets got from the safe to the police laboratory. The chain of evidence was broken, and there was no proof that the bullets tested were the same bullets Hiss said he removed from Rabin's body. And there is yet another unsolvable difficulty. Dr. Kluger also testified that he was the one that removed the bullets from Rabin. Both doctors can't be right.

However contradictory the testimony regarding custody and delivery of the bullets is, consider the fate of the gun itself.

Here is the testimony of Police Supervisor Yamin Yitzhak, head of the anti-terrorism unit at the rally.

Yitzhak: I was coming down the stairs behind the stage. I was two or three steps from the bottom when I heard three shots in a row. I ran quickly down. I saw a guy in a blue shirt holding a black gun and I jumped on him. Seconds passed between the shots and when I apprehended the guy. I hit him in his hand, pulled his hair, and wrestled him to the ground. Then others joined in. The gun was still in his hand.

Court: From the moment of physical contact, there were no other shots?

Yitzhak: After then, no. The gun was cocked, the clip was inside. I grabbed the defendant's right hand, knowing the hammer of the gun was cocked. I twisted his hand and took the gun from him quickly. Someone from the service [Shabak] arrived and asked me for the gun, I refused to hand it over, and a give-me-the-gun war erupted. I was holding on to the gun while my thumb was blocking the hammer. The Shabak agent insisted I give him the gun and I said no, because it wasn't disarmed. I was surrounded by people and I shouted at them to cuff him [Amir] ... After he was taken away, the Shabak guy persisted in harassing me. I went looking for the area commander and asked him to get this guy off my back. He was a Shabak agent but I don't know his name. All the while, he was trying to get the gun. After the defendant was pinned to the wall, I showed the gun to the area commander. I took it aside to check it. I removed the bullet from the chamber and it fell to the ground where I couldn't see it. I asked for a nylon bag, put the gun and clip in it and shoved it into the front of my pants. After a search of the area was organized, I gave the gun to the investigations officer, Deputy Inspector Naftali.

Defense: How far away from the defendant were you when you heard the shots?

Yitzhak: About from here to the defense table (three meters).

Defense: And the defendant was still standing when you got to him.

Yitzhak: He was still standing. There was someone beside him wearing a grey shirt or jacket.

At this point, Yigal Amir had had enough. He cross-examined Yitzhak with vigor. He held out his right hand as if a gun was in it and asked Yitzhak to demonstrate how he took the gun from him. The demonstration was different than his testimony. Instead of pulling his hair, he knocked Amir in the nape with his right hand and grabbed the gun with his left. He justified the awkward position by explaining that he was ambidextrous. Amir burst out in anger.

Amir: You say you took the gun from me. I say it fell on the ground and I heard it as it landed.

Yitzhak: I'm positive I took it.

Amir (to the court): There were two guards accompanying the Prime Minister. And you say they did not try to apprehend me until you ran all the way from the steps. That sounds weird.

Yitzhak: I think the distance between the place the bodyguards were and where I was, I was on the way down the steps and the distance was reduced, I just remember there were other people there, I took the gun from you, for sure. I punched you, for sure. I know what I did. Maybe there were other people with me. They came, it was a matter of seconds, no, less. If someone else was there, he neglected to take the weapon. I did that. I didn't see the Prime Minister but I was really close to him. Really close.

Third year law student Amir had succeeded in totally rattling Yitzhak.

Amir: Maybe you picked it up off the ground and thought you took it from me?

Yitzhak: No.

Amir: People jumped on me, then there were two shots. Lots of people jumped at the same time. I dropped the gun so they wouldn't shoot me. I heard the sound of it hitting the ground.

Yitzhak: No. I can tell you definitely that first I heard three shots and in a matter of seconds, after the three shots, I got to you, dropped you on the ground and took your gun.

Defense: You say you did what you did but maybe he really did release the gun first.

Yitzhak: I'll say it again, from the moment I saw the guy, it was seconds until I took the gun from him.

Supervisor Yitzhak insists he took Amir's gun from his hand. He recalls the moment in great detail including in his testimony the fact that he placed his thumb between the hammer and cartridge, disarmed the gun and gave it to Officer Naftali. And while all this was going on, one Shabak agent was desperately trying to get him to hand the gun over to him.

His testimony certainly casts a veil of suspicion over Shabak agents' accounts. Yitzhak maintained that he ran from three meter's distance, a matter of seconds, and Amir was still on his feet. This is in direct contradiction to all previous testimony, including Amir's. He said Amir shot three times without any interference from Rabin's bodyguards. And he insisted that the gun he wrestled from Amir was the gun that did the shooting. So why would the Shabak be so desperate to keep it out of the hands of the police? The answer, if Yitzhak was telling the truth, is that the police examiner would discover that Amir shot only once, and that the bullets in Rabin's body didn't match this gun.

Compare Yitzhak's testimony to that of other witnesses.

* Shabak officer Adi Azulai related in his police statement of the night of the murder that he saw the gun fall, that HE found the gun on the ground, that there was a bullet in the chamber and that a police officer took it from him.
* Police unit officer Avi Cohen reported, the same night, that he saw the gun fall as Amir was pounced on.
* An unnamed Police officer from the Yarkon district headquarters reported, the same night, that he also saw the gun fall.
* Officer Yisrael Gabai of the Yarkon district headquarters, testified at Amir's trial that he saw Yamin Yitzhak take the gun from Amir's hand.

- Deputy Inspector Naftali testified that other policemen told him they took the gun from Amir. In the same session, he added that a watch and pair of glasses were found on the ground at the murder scene and their owners have never been found.
- Police Officer Yisrael Gabai testified that he saw the gun taken from Amir's hand.
- Shabak agent "Shin" (Sh) testified that agent "Bet" (B) Benny Lahav, a high ranking Shabak official, demanded the gun from Yamin Yitzhak.
- Shabak agent "Aleph" (A) testified that he saw the argument between "Bet," Lahav and the policeman holding the gun. Lahav wanted the gun but the policeman wouldn't give it to him. Lahav examined the gun, checked the bullets and returned it to the policeman.
- Police officer Avi Yahav testified that he saw a policeman holding the gun, saying it was Amir's.
- Police officer Efron Moshe testified that the gun was on the ground and the police picked it up.
- Police officer Avraham Cohen initially testified that the gun was forced out of Amir's hand, then he retracted his words, testifying that Amir dropped the gun. He concluded that Deputy Inspector Naftali eventually got possession of it.

There you have it. Two Shabak officers backed Yamin Yitzhak's testimony about fighting over the gun with a high-ranking Shabak official. Four policemen testified that either Yitzhak or another police officer wrestled the gun out of Amir's hand. On the other hand, one Shabak agent claimed he found the gun on the ground and three policemen testified that the gun fell to the ground.

So who are you going to believe? All of them if there was a second gun. Those few researchers who have examined the evidence closely are divided over when the fatal bullets were shot. Those who believe Rabin was murdered in his car or at the hospital point to: the car door closing before anyone was supposed to be inside, the unexplainably long ride to the hospital; the police lab tests proving there were two point blank or near point blank shots at the back; the account of Yevgeny Furman to Reuters that he saw Rabin in the emergency room of Ichilov with a chest wound, and the doctors who reported a third chest wound.

Those who insist he was shot at the parking lot of the rally stress the three shots heard by many people, and the ample, contradictory testimony of police and Shabak officers just reviewed which indicates to them the likelihood of a second gun at the scene of the murder. The truth may yet turn out to be a combination of both scenarios.

Chapter Nineteen
THE THIRD SHOT AT RABIN

The conspiracy to shoot Yitzhak Rabin was finally proved. According to the Shamgar Commission Report, the testimony at the trial of Yigal Amir, and the Kempler film, Yigal Amir shot Rabin twice in the back. But, what if Rabin had a third wound in the chest that Amir could not have done from behind?

Natan Gefen showed me a copy of the last page of a report signed by Dr. Mordecai Gutman at 11:30 PM on Ichilov Hospital stationery. Regarding Rabin's wounds Dr. Gutman wrote, "Bullet wound in upper lung lobe of 2.5–3 cm. Exit wound in the direction of D5-6 with a shattering of the vertebrae."

The document was a remarkable discovery. For one thing, until then I had found no other source that mentioned that Rabin's spinal cord had been shattered. I called a friend—a respected physician. (The name of the physician and his wife must be deleted for legal reasons. She works for the police and cannot reveal her identity.) Dr. Gutman's report, he wrote, "What is being described is a shot to the chest which entered and exited the lung, shattering vertebrae numbers D5-6 in the upper back."

Could such a wound have been caused by a shot to the back? "Not likely. To do so, the bullet would have had to have entered the back, pierced the upper lobe of the lung, then returned to exit the lung before smashing into the backbone. Bullets have been known to take unexpected paths, but on first consideration, this doesn't seem feasible."

I was totally stumped by the report since it contradicted the honest testimony of Chief Lieutentant Baruch Gladstein of the Israel Police Fibers and Materials Laboratory at the trial of Yigal Amir. After examining Rabin's suit and shirt, he determined that the Prime Minister was shot twice in the back from point blank and near point blank range. He would not have missed a bullethole in the chest nor, after what he revealed would he likely have lied in court about it.

I referred Gefen to two journalists, Boaz Gaon of *Maariv* and Jay Bushinksky of NBC. Both took the document to Ichilov where hospital officials confirmed its veracity. However, they added, according to Bushinsky, a cautionary explanation that, "This is the last page of a six page medical procedural report which was intended only for the perusal of Rabin's immediate family. Without understanding the first five pages, the last page is out of context and meaningless."

Gutman's handwritten report was never released to anyone except Leah Rabin. Instead, a typed report signed by Drs. Gutman, Hausner and Kluger was released publicly two days after the assassination. Film director Merav Ktorza and her partner, cameraman Alon Eilat, received the full report from Natan Gefen on May 14, 1996. The physician and his medic wife, with much experience dealing directly with bullet wounds, joined me at Merav and Aloni's home in Bet Shemesh for a professional reading of: Dr. Gutman's report; the public procedural report; the pathologist's summation; and the court testimony of the surgeon, Dr. Kluger, and the pathologist, Dr. Hiss.

The very first line of Dr. Gutman's report states that Rabin was brought into the emergency room with "no pulse or heartbeat and suffering from priapism." The physician immediately explained, "Priapism means he had a severe injury to his nervous system."

The next day he faxed me a page from a medical report which read: "In the male, check for priapism (sustained erection of the penis), which, when present, is a characteristic sign of spinal cord injury."

The medic noted, "To me, this is proof that the report is genuine. Considering the sensitivity of the nation at that moment, no doctor would have reported priapism unless he was being honest in his observations."

However, I add, that almost two months later, Dr. David Chayan, who was investigating the medical reports, told me, "Drop the priapism aspect. Rabin was suffering from a condition that would explain it." Later, two other doctors informed me that Rabin had a penile implant which could well explain the priapism.

The report then described procedures which succeeded in reviving Rabin. His pulse and heartbeat returned and he was rushed to the operating room where his padding was removed. Damage caused by a bullethole from the right upper lung which shattered vertebrae D5-6 was described. A bullet wound of the flank which passed through the spleen and lodged in the lower left lung was also noted. The latter wound caused little bleeding and was not fatal. A total of eight units of blood were transfused during the operation. The wound to the chest and spinal cord ultimately was the cause of death. Despite Ichilov's later protest, there was nothing out of context in the final page of Dr. Gutman's report. He described a chest wound whose path led to a shattered spinal cord.

The surgeon, Dr. Gutman, signed his report at 11:30 PM of November 4. The pathologist, Dr. Hiss, began work on Rabin's body approximately two hours later. Then a most remarkable change took place; the priaspism, chest wound and shattered spinal cord disappeared. He concluded that, "There was no damage to the spinal cord." Both he and Dr. Kluger so testified at the trial of Yigal Amir in March, 1996.

The joint public report of Drs. Gutman, Hausner and Kluger two days later concurred with Dr. Hiss: no priapism, no chest wound, and especially, no shattered vertebrae. Vertebrae 5-6 became rib numbers 5 and 6. The new version of events had Rabin shot in the back, the bullet passing between ribs 5-6 and lodging in the upper lobe of the right lung.

So what happened between 11:30 and 1:30?

What to do about the contradiction between Chief Lieutenant Gladstein's report of two bullets through the back of Rabin's clothing and Dr. Gutman's description of a fatal chest wound?

On May 2, 1997, I received a visit from the researcher of this book, an energetic young man, Yechiel Mann, who had previously e-mailed me that he had been gathering evidence since the very night of the assassination. He left me a videotape of Channel One's coverage of the assassination that he had had the foresight to record on the night of the murder. It was almost four hours long and I put it aside for future reference.

The next Friday evening, I received a visit from Zeev Barcella, the editor of the *Vesti,* and a staff reporter Emma Sodnikov. Joining us, quite accidentally, was a family friend, a Russian born pharmacist, Assia Miller.

During the interview, I gave Zeev Natan Gefen's phone number and described the document he had uncovered. Zeev related a relevant story:

"The morning after the assassination, a Russian-speaking operating room nurse called me and said, 'There's something wrong. The media isn't reporting Rabin's real wounds. His spine was shattered and they're saying it wasn't.' Ninety minutes later she called me back sounding terrified and told me, 'I didn't call you before. You never heard from me,' and then she put down the phone."

I decided to present Zeev with the most perplexing piece of evidence I had acquired. In one of the most bizarre episodes of the assassination night, while Rabin was being operated on, his aide Eitan Haber rifled through Rabin's pockets, pulling out whatever was inside. Among the items he recovered, was a bloody song sheet Rabin had placed in his chest pocket. Within the bloodstain was a black, nearly perfectly round stain that looked like a hole.

I had gone on television the previous October and claimed there was a bullethole in the sheet of paper. Unfortunately for me, the sheet was folded in four and the hole was in only one section. The television reporter jumped on the error, claimed the hole was a bloodstain and I lost a lot of credibility.

But, as Assia noted, that hole-like stain was no bloodstain. Blood isn't black nor does it clot in near perfect circles the size of a bullet. Zeev guessed, "It looks like someone tried to burn a hole into the sheet, then thought better of it and stopped." Emma concurred, "That would explain the black color."

Bullethole or not, the bloody song sheet more than merely indicated that Rabin was bleeding from the chest. Two weeks later my physician friend explained, "It's just not likely that a back wound would be absorbed from paper in the chest pocket." So how did the blood get on the sheet?

On May 11, I received a remarkable document. It was an appeal submitted to the Supreme Court of Israel on March 6, 1996. Within, a taxi driver felt, as a good citizen, that he had to relay important testimony concerning the Rabin assassination. I add, the taxi driver sought no publicity, his name remains unknown to the public and people do not present evidence to the Supreme Court on a lark. I further add, the conclusions of the Supreme Court's session regarding the following testimony has never been released to the public.

Included in the request to submit new evidence are the following passages:

Preliminary: According to the declaration of the witness, the Prime Minister was shot by a third bullet of a different caliber from the other two bullets.

I.T. (full name hidden because the witness fears retaliation) declare the following to be truthful:

On March 27, 1996 the verdict in the trial of Yigal Amir was read.

> I am a taxi driver and at the time the verdict was announced over the radio, I was driving a tanned passenger, about 50 years old with silver-rimmed glasses from Yaffa to Ichilov Hospital in Tel Aviv.
>
> After hearing the Amir verdict, the passenger began a conversation with me. He said Yigal Amir was right and according to the facts he couldn't have killed the Prime Minister even if he wanted to.
>
> I asked the passenger what he meant and he said one bullet was shot from less than 20 cm away, the other, even closer and a third bullet of a different caliber was shot point blank.
>
> I told him those facts weren't published anywhere and that I didn't believe him. At this point the passenger showed me his identity card which read that he was a pathologist. I have forgotten his name but it might be Peretz.
>
> I was surprised to see he was a pathologist and then he told me he examined Rabin's body on the night of the murder.

I said that on the night of the murder, another pathologist announced on television that Rabin was shot by two bullets. I asked him if it's possible that after the announcement someone could have got to the operating room and shot Rabin again. The passenger didn't answer me but he smiled. I asked him if he was certain there were three bullets and he replied he examined Rabin's body and found three entrance wounds.

During the course of the journey, the passenger told me that there was another dead body in the hospital that night and that according to his clothing and other signs he was positive it was of a bodyguard from the event that night. He told me that the government wasn't telling the whole story. He added that there was something about the Prime Minister's clothes they weren't telling either but he didn't elaborate.

That is my testimony and it is the truth.

The witness describes Yehuda Hiss, a 50-year-old man with silver framed glasses. A quick glance at the three Hebrew letters that spell Peretz can look like the three letters in Hiss. More to the point, Hiss was the only pathologist to examine Rabin. The witness also describes the findings of chief Lieutenant Baruch Gladstein and the "suicide" of Yaov Kuriel rather exactly for a mere cab driver.

On May 12, I was rereading the transcripts of Yigal Amir's trial and was startled by the testimony of Rabin's bodyguard Yoram Rubin. While Rabin was in the operating room, his driver Menachem Damti rushed up to the "wounded" bodyguard Yoram Rubin and took his gun from him. Rubin testified that, "I gave it to him because I wasn't myself and I was worried that someone, an Arab or another minority member would take it." One would not expect many Arabs to be admitted to the area where the Prime Minister and his bodyguard were situated. I couldn't understand why Rubin handed his gun to Damti, nor what he needed it for at that moment. Rubin's gun was never mentioned again.

On May 15, I finally watched Yechial's videotape of Channel One's coverage of the assassination night. At about 11:30, the director of Ichilov Hospital, Dr. Gabi Barabash announced the cause of Rabin's death: "The Prime Minister arrived at the hospital without pulse or heartbeat. He was clinically dead. We succeeded in reviving him and transfused 21 units of blood but the wounds were too severe and he succumbed to them."

"What were the wounds?" asked the television reporter Chaim Yavin.

"There was a wound to the spleen and a gaping hole in the chest leading to the backbone. The first bullet was not necessarily fatal. The other bullet tore apart vessels leading to the heart and shattered his spinal cord ... The Prime Minister died of spinal shock."

At 12:30, Health Minister Ephraim Sneh appeared on television and pronounced the cause of Rabin's death. He prefaced the announcement with the words, "As a result of incitement, Prime Minister Rabin died tonight ... He took three bullets, one in the chest, one in the stomach and one in the spine."

What Sneh was reporting was a second spine injury. Besides the chest wound which resulted in two vertebrae shattered, Sneh reported another bullet wound to the spine. That would have explained Rabin's priapism in the emergency room.

At 11:30, the director general of Ichilov Hospital announced that Rabin was shot twice. An hour later, the Minister of Health, surely in an informed, official capacity announced a third bullet. But both were in agreement on two essential facts: Rabin was shot in the chest and his spinal cord was shattered. These facts were never again mentioned. By the next day and henceforth, the official story was that Yigal Amir shot Rabin in the back twice injuring his flank, waist, spleen and lungs. But never, not in the Shamgar Report nor at Amir's trial is there a word about a chest wound or shattered spine. If those were the wounds, Amir would have had to have shot from the front and Rabin would have collapsed on the spot from the severed nerves. The Kempler film shows Amir shooting from behind and Rabin continuing to walk after the first shot.

I sat there thinking. Over and over I considered that Yigal Amir shot from behind. He could not have caused the chest wound. But what of Chief Lieutenant Gladstein's testimony that Rabin's clothing bore the holes of only two shots, neither from the front?

Direct evidence of a third shot now came from many sources including: the health minister; the patient Yevgeny Furman; the Director General of Ichilov Hospital; testimony to the Supreme

Court; the taxi driver; Dr. Gutman's signed report; and from the
nurse who called Zeev Barcella. The evidence was overwhelming.
There had to have been a third shot from the front. But how?

Then it hit me. I called Alon Eilat and said, "Eureka. [Cliché or
not, I really quoted Archimedes]. I know how it happened."

He rushed over and looked at the filmed testimony of Sneh and
Barabash for the first time. He said in reaction, "You can't get
higher level testimony than that. There had to have been a chest
wound."

"So," I asked, "What about Gladstein's evidence based on two
bullets in the back of Rabin's suit?"

Alon thought hard and finally gave up.

I said, "The only possibility is that Rabin wasn't wearing his
clothes when he was shot in the chest. It had to have been done in
the hospital."

We went over the evidence and came up with the most likely scenario. Rabin arrived alive at the hospital. He took two point blank
shots in the back during the car ride to Ichilov, including one to the
spine and somehow survived them. When the doctors revived him,
the conspirators panicked and used one of their guns to finish him
off with a bullet through the chest which shattered his spine again.

It was at this point that the cover-up began. The conspirators
realized the fatal flaw in the final shot. Rabin wasn't wearing his
clothes and there was no hole in the front of his suit or shirt. So they
rifled through his pockets, found the song sheet and tried to burn a
bullet hole through it, probably with a cigarette. Quickly, they realized how futile that was and abandoned the idea. There was no
believable way to add a third shot to the clothes or their contents.

Instead, they coerced the doctors and staff to lie. One can only
imagine the brutal threats. We had a hint of them in May, 1995
when the news magazine *Zman Tel Aviv* reported that everyone on
duty at Ichilov treating Rabin, 17 people, received anonymous death
threats by mail. The first to be threatened that night was the pathologist and the possible taxi passenger Dr. Hiss. By 2 AM, he got rid of
the truthful conclusions of Drs. Gutman, Sneh and Barabash and
invented a whole new story deleting the chest and spinal wounds.
And from that point on, the cover-up continued. Murder threats
from people who have nothing to lose can keep a lot of people quiet,

even and especially cabinet ministers. It seemed like the perfect scenario, until a week later when I received a copy of the *Jerusalem Post* of November 5, 1995, the morning of the assassination.

Shimon Peres, who a year later told *Yediot Ahronot* that he had been inside the operating room and had seen "Rabin, naked on the table, his face blue and puffy from being pushed onto the pavement," reported to the *Post* that, "The last song he sang at the rally was 'The Song Of Peace.' He put the songsheet in his pocket and the bullet went through this song."

Alon tried brushing the quote off-rationalizing, "Maybe Peres was being dramatic, that he didn't literally mean the bullet went through the sheet."

Perhaps, but Yevgeny Furman's testimony was tougher to explain. He told the *Post* that he was a patient in the emergency room. "Security guards ran in suddenly and said, 'Clear the room. Rabin has been hit.' He was lying on his side and there was a big blood stain on his chest."

Alon's explanation was that Furman may have seen Rabin "as he was being moved from the emergency room to the operating theatre." As useful as that explanation would have been, Furman says nothing to back it.

The exact circumstances of Rabin's death may remain a mystery until an eyewitness finds the courage to speak out. However, five people who saw him in the operating theater, Drs. Sneh, Gutman and Barabash, as well as Peres and the unnamed Russian speaking nurse, said he was shot through the chest from the front. And that is testimony that should have stood up in any court.

Chapter Twenty
RABIN MURDER EYEWITNESS COMES FORWARD

Friday, September 26, 1997, was a banner day for the truth. *Yediot Ahronot's* weekend magazine chain published a four page exposé of the government cover-up of Avishai Raviv's activities prior to the Rabin assassination.

The author of the article, Gadi Blum, wrote that the Attorney General Edna Arbel was deliberately hiding the findings of two government inquiries, led by Erin Shendar and Michael Eitan into Raviv's role in the assassination. Further, the article contended that Amir was being manipulated to stop the movement to arrest and question Raviv (i.e., he demanded that his mother withdraw a petition to the Supreme Court to have Raviv investigated).

The article was very respectful towards me, calling me the "father of the Rabin conspiracy theory, which is given great credibility in Judea and Samaria." However, one quote was inaccurate. I told Mr. Blum that I had been invited to a minister's office where his advisor informed me that the highest levels of the Likud secretly used the truth about the assassination against Labour in the previous election campaign. As Blum told it, I received my information from the minister himself. Despite the blunder, this article remains a most important stepping stone toward the final revelation of what really happened to Rabin the night he was murdered.

One person who read the article with great interest was Mordi Yisrael. He is the man on the Kempler film who Amir circled to get a clear shot at Rabin.* He stood just in front of Amir and was closest to Rabin when the shot was fired. Yet, until this article was released, he had been no more than a minor character in the play. That was about to change. A day after he read Blum's piece, he tracked me down and we met the next morning.

I had already come to know him by face, having seen him hundreds of times on the Kempler film. I heard rather sinister rumours about his alleged role in the murder. The rumours started as a result of the stills from the Kempler film released to *Yediot Ahronot*. Recall that on one still another person was superimposed over Amir's picture. So sloppy a job, in fact, that Amir is seen shooting with his left hand, though all witnesses saw him shoot with his right. This

---

* In late 1997, *Anashim* magazine printed an interview with Mordi Yisrael which made me somewhat reluctant to include this chapter. He said he was sure he had convinced me that there was no conspiracy and he had denied telling me that the gunshots sounded like "party poppers." That said, I insist that I accurately recorded his version of events and stand by what is written. Further, a London TV producer spoke to Mordi the day after I interviewed him and he related the same story to him.

altered photo made it appear that Amir's arm was supported on Mordi Yisrael's shoulder. Hence the whispered rumours that he was an accomplice. I never took such talk seriously but I did take note that Mordi Yisrael was becoming an entrenched figure in the legend slowly being constructed around the Rabin murder.

Mordi is in his mid-20s and lives with his parents in a fourth floor apartment in Kiryat Gat. His mother was sympathetic, but father is a police investigator and objected to Mordi talking to me. "You are being interrogated again," he says. Mordi replies, "I'm just trying to figure out what happened. I have to know already."

On the evening of November 4, 1995, Mordi was on assignment for the Tel Aviv College where he was a media student. He was to tape as many politicians as he could for a mock radio report. "I had everything on tape," he says. "The machine was rolling right through the assassination. I was just behind Rabin, holding the mike and calling to him to offer a comment. In the cab on the way home I thought to myself that I recorded a historical event. But when I got home, nothing was on the tape. It was all fuzz. I've used the machine hundreds of times before and it always recorded. I couldn't understand why it didn't record at all. I would have noticed if the mike was pulled out."

Before delving into Mordi's recollection of the evening, it is advisable to review the Shamgar Commission's account of the event. The official version has Amir shooting Rabin in the back from the 50 cm range. Immediately after, bodyguard Yoram Rubin fell on Rabin and covered him. While both were prone on the ground, Amir, though held by two other bodyguards, managed to shoot, first Rubin and then Rabin from about 20 cm directly above them.

Here is what Mordi Yisrael, the eyewitness closest to the murder scene, recalls.

"As I arrived backstage I asked a policeman if I could get past the barrier. He let me in without checking my person or tape recorder. At the time I thought this was really lax of him, and later I thought it was this kind of laxness that caused the murder. Now, I'm not so sure I wasn't deliberately allowed in. I say that because I was the only journalist around. There should have been lots of reporters questioning Rabin, but I was the only one. Just recently it began occurring to me that maybe there was a mixup, and I was let in because my description, short, young 20s, Sephardic, in short-sleeve shirt, matched Amir's.

"As soon as I was in, I began interviewing the politicians roaming around the area. Then I saw Peres coming down the steps and decided to get him on tape. But he was acting very strangely. Instead of walking at a normal pace to his car, he darted straight at the crowd. I had to rush to keep up with him. Right then, I thought that something was wrong. Why was he in such a hurry and why did he expose himself to the crowd like that? He took no precautions when meeting the people, yet he wasn't friendly to them either. He shook a few hands and left. I managed to ask him how he thought the rally went and he answered, 'Very successfully,' before he took off."

At this point, we watched the relevant section of the Kempler film. Yisrael pointed himself out talking to Peres and I stressed that Peres then rushed straight to Rabin's car and stopped opposite it. While Peres was examining the vehicle with four Shabak agents, there was the break in the film. Then Peres is seen talking with Rabin's driver, Menachem Damti. Yisrael was impressed. "Why was Peres in such a rush to look at Rabin's car?" he asked.

After succeeding in taping a perfunctory quote from Peres, Yisrael saw Rabin descending the steps. He decided to capture him on tape as well. This would make his assignment a complete success. He approached the Prime Minister from behind and beseeched him to make a few remarks to his mike.

"Even then I noticed how easy it was to get to Rabin. I saw his rear bodyguard stop in his tracks to have a few words with a policeman. Rabin was totally uncovered and I just stepped up to him. He was ignoring my questions and walking at a fast clip. Finally, I got his attention and he turned around to answer me. Then I heard the shot. He turned to me simultaneously with the shot. But, I don't think either of us thought there was any danger, since the noise wasn't like a gun shot, rather like a harmless party popper."

He had answered one of the more nagging questions of the murder mystery: why did Rabin, and only Rabin, react to the shot by turning his head toward it? Until then, I had postulated that Rabin was the only one to feel the blast from the blank bullet and thus was the first to react. It wasn't a satisfying answer. That he was coincidentally turning to speak to Yisrael made much more sense. Yisrael stops the conversation, saying, "There's something in the film that bothers me." He fast-forwarded the video and replayed the moment. "It didn't happen that fast," he said. "In the film Rabin turns his head in a split second. In reality, he turned to me at a perfectly normal speed."

Yisrael had now verified one of the central claims made by Rabin murder researcher Natan Gefen. Gefen insisted proof that the Kempler film was doctored existed in the speed in which Rabin reacted to the first shot. Rabin turned his head around just .25 of a second after the shot was fired. The typical reaction speed of a man thirty years younger is .75 of a second. Said Gefen, "Rabin reacted three times faster to the shot than a much younger man typically would. And Rabin was not James Bond. He drank and wasn't fit. There is no way he would have reacted to the sound before any of his bodyguards."

Yisrael reached the dramatic climax. "Immediately after the shot, I heard someone shout from the crowd, 'They're blanks. They're blanks.' Just as Rabin and I made eye-contact, Rabin's face suddenly displayed utter terror. He lifted his hands to eye-level, stared over my shoulder for a split-second and then he hunched his shoulders and tried to run away. He was bent over as I turned around and saw Amir standing all by himself with his arm extended, pistol in hand. Then he shot twice in a row. I saw the blasts from both shots. But, neither sounded like real gunshots; again, more like party poppers.

"Then I turned back and saw Rabin. It was pathetic. He was all alone, not a bodyguard near him, while Amir was shooting. He saw Amir, but had nowhere to run. After the two shots were fired, his bodyguards finally jumped on him."

Mordi Yisrael testified to the Shamgar Commission, but his testimony was completely ignored. You won't find Mordi Yisrael's name in the publicly released findings of the commission, though it might have turned up in the 30% of the report that was hidden. Yisrael has never read either report and like most Israelis, doesn't know how far reaching this conspiracy truly is.

So I pulled out some files and showed them to him for his reaction. First I showed him bodyguard Yoram Rubin's testimony to Shamgar: "I jumped on the Prime Minister, heard a shot, and felt a jolt of electricity rush through my arm. Then I heard another shot, I waited for a hiatus in the shooting, and then said, "Yitzhak, can you hear me and only me, goddammit."

Yisrael asked, "Is he saying he got shot on the ground and then Rabin?"

"Yes," I replied. "According to the official version, Rabin took the first shot from 50-70 cm while standing up, Rubin took the next shot from 20 cm while prone and then Rabin took a similar shot."

"You mean Amir got closer for the last two shots?"

"Yes."

"Absolutely out of the question. There was a long gap between the first two shots, maybe three or four seconds. During that time, Rabin ran away from Amir while he stood still. Rabin was a good two meters away from Amir when he was shot again. And, I repeat what I just said, Rabin was hunched over, not lying, all alone. Not Rubin, nor anyone else was covering him, so Rubin could not possibly have been shot by Amir. He is mistaken about everything."

I showed him driver Menachem Damti's testimony to Shamgar: "I heard the shot just as I was opening the door for Leah Rabin. The Prime Minister fell just half a meter from the car."

"Leah Rabin," Yisrael recalls, "was nowhere near the car. And Rabin fell a good two meters from the car. Damti is so mistaken it sounds like he's lying."

Next I offer him documents hidden from the public: Chief Lieutenant Gladstein's findings that Rabin was shot point blank, Dr. Guttman's report that Rabin was shot through the chest and spine and Bernard Shechter's ballistics report that has Amir's gun shooting just once. I assure and reassure him that all the documents were real.

"These reports are describing another murder," he notes. "Rabin's spine couldn't have been shattered, he kept walking way from Amir. Amir never shot point blank; I saw the three gun blasts and I witnessed him taking two of the shots. He never got close to point blank range and the last two shots were from two meters away. If the ballistics report is accurate they had to have been examining another gun."

By now, Yisrael was flummoxed. He was on the front line of the murder. He had a better view than anyone else. He was positioned to see the assassination from both the killer and the victim's point of view. Yet the Shangar Commission told a story that had nothing to do with the truth as he saw it. Perhaps most troubling to him were the police and medical reports which describe an entirely different murder, one in which Rabin is shot point blank and from the front.

Though Yisrael's description of the gun shots sounding like party poppers later was recanted in the *Anashim* article, he did repeat almost verbatim the most important issues. He contracted the Shamgar Commission finding by saying again that Rubin did not pounce on him, and Amir did not move closer to Rabin for the second and third shots.

"You know," he says. "There was a lot more I didn't tell you. Much stranger things. I'm not ready to tell them to anyone yet." We look at the Kempler film again. There is Yisrael and there is Amir's gun. We see the blast and then watch Yisrael flinch and duck. "Instead of flinching," he asks, "what would have happened if I had grabbed Amir's arm and wrestled him to the ground?"

"My guess," I answered, "is you'd be well on the road to a successful political career by now."

Chapter Twenty One
MISCELLANEOUS MYSTERIES

After over 18 months of research, the proof of a conspiracy to murder Yitzhak Rabin was nearly in hand. A few loose ends would have to be tied and then the case would close like a finely wrapped gift. I sent my researcher, Yechiel Mann, to the national newspaper archive, Beit Ariellah, to find citations for two bothersome mysteries. The first assignment was to find an article that I was repeatedly told appeared in *Maariv* two months after the murder. In it, the reporter provides proof that Yigal Amir was arrested on June 27, 1995 on suspicion of planning Rabin's murder and released on July 1 on the orders of the Shabak. This proof came in the form of three letters between the police and Shabak.

The second assignment was especially important. I was looking for backup sources that substantiated my assertion that the Chief

Surgeon of Ichilov, Dr. Yehuda Skornik, had said that based on gunpowder traces found in Rabin's wounds, and the shape of the
wounds themselves, Rabin was shot point blank.

The trip to the archives was a flop. Yechiel found likely refer-
ences, but when he opened the newspapers to find the stories, they
had been cut out. He had found an article on the doctors of Ichilov
ripped in two, only half of which was readable, with the half with
information on Dr. Skornik missing.

Though the articles were eventually uncovered from another
source the next week, Yechiel returned to Bet Ariellah. This time he
was met by a woman in her 20s who had a file on the assassination
ready for him. She explained that she was doing research on the subject, but would not explain how she knew why he was there.

The mystery lady provided some useful peripheral information,
but the hard data on Skornik could not be found. It seemed his file
had been erased from the computer. The Chief Surgeon of Ichilov
no longer existed in Bet Ariellah's hard drive. Not a single quote,
even those regarding unrelated incidents from traffic accidents, were
available.

My researcher still managed to find some intriguing information.
He left the archives with photocopies of articles supplied by the
helpful woman and a few juicy finds of his own.

These articles, however, were unwelcome. Just when I thought I
was finally approaching something resembling an airtight scenario,
new mysteries emerged that would require plausible explanations ...
perhaps in a follow-up book. I had to admit, the assassination was
too complicated to be solved completely, and new information just
wouldn't stop coming in.

Questions evolving from those newspaper discoveries include:

What Does Dr. Yehuda Skornik Know And Why Isn't He Telling?

As Chief Surgeon of Ichilov Hospital, Dr. Skornik was not only
privy to Rabin's medical records, but was obliged to read every word
written by his surgeons about their treatment of him on that final
night of his life. Yet, he did not testify at the Shamgar Commission
nor at Amir's trial.

We called Ichilov Hospital several times to speak to Dr. Skornik.

His calls were screened by his secretary who wouldn't allow one call through. "Dr. Skornik is a very busy man," was the only explanation. Why all the secrecy?

On the night of the assassination, Dr. Skornik's son, Ohad, was arrested and charged with being an accessory to Rabin's murder. The scenario is a bit too bizarre. While Skornik's staff was working to save Rabin, the Chief Surgeon's son was being sought in connection to Rabin's murder. The police suspected that Ohad, a friend of Yigal Amir's from Bar Ilan University, withheld prior knowledge of the assassination. Five days later, he was released from jail.

I asked myself, what are the odds of this?

Why Couldn't The Doctors Get Their Stories Straight?

Until my researcher brought in his batch of printed trouble for me, I had believed that the Shamgar Commission, based on its findings, knew nothing of Rabin's spinal cord injury. But, buried in an article about the driver Damti's testimony to the commission, is Professor Gabi Barabash's testimony. It read: "The first bullet caused injury to Rabin's vertebrae and the spinal cord."

The Shamgar Commission was informed, so why didn't they ask the next, most obvious questions: Was the spinal cord badly damaged, and if so, why is Rabin seen on the Kempler film walking after the shot?

As if I didn't need more proof that Rabin was shot in the spine and chest, the following article appeared in *Maariv* on the day after the murder. Reporters Yossi Levy, Yaacov Galanti and Shira Imerglick wrote, "According to expert sources, the first bullet struck Rabin in the chest and the second in the spinal cord ... Amir shot from a distance of two or three meters." Though the order of injury and shooting range were muddled, those experts did confirm that the crucial wounds were to the chest and spine.

If Dr. Barabash testified to a spinal wound at Amir's trial, then his testimony never appeared in the transcripts. Two other prominent doctors with relevant information also did not testify at the trial; Dr. Mordechai Gutman, whose original report has Rabin shot in the chest from the front, and the aforementioned Dr. Yehuda Skornik.

But, there was yet another doctor who disappeared from the legal arena, and until the stack of clippings arrived from Bet Ariella, I had never heard of him. On November 6, 1995, *Maariv* reporter Yisraela Shaked interviewed Dr. Nir Cohen, a surgical expert who was on duty at the trauma center of the hospital at 9:52 PM and was the first to tend to Rabin. "Only after two minutes of resuscitation did I realize the man I was treating was the Prime Minister," he said.

"I recall hearing a different sounding siren. Immediately after, I saw him transferred from the ambulance to the trauma room. He was pale, had no pulse, and was deeply gasping. After beginning resuscitation, I put all the pieces together when I saw his fancy suit, and the bodyguard yelling as he came in, 'This is a disaster. This is a disaster.' Then the reports arrived by phone and pager that Rabin was on the way to us. They arrived as Rabin was being resuscitated."

We can forgive Dr. Cohen for his one minute error on the time of arrival. But, Rabin did not arrive in an ambulance. And it's most unlikely he could mistake a black limousine for an ambulance. Dr. Cohen may not be telling the truth. Rabin was not shot in the face, and it's unbelievable that Dr. Cohen would not recognize him immediately. That he eventually figured out who he was by his fancy suit and his screaming bodyguard is implausible. What is not implausible is that the hospital was only told of Rabin's imminent arrival well after Dr. Cohen had begun treating him. Within this piece of truth may be the reason Dr. Cohen lied, unconvincingly, to *Maariv.*

How Did Damti Get Away With So Many Lies?
Menachem Damti was not supposed to be Rabin's chauffeur on the night of his death. He was a last second replacement for Rabin's regular driver, Yeheskal Sharabi. The real reason for the decision to replace Sharabi with Damti is not hard to imagine, what is difficult to fathom is how much Damti was allowed to perjure himself.

Let us compare Damti's ever-changing version of reality with the facts. Shortly after the murder, Damti told television reporter Rafi Reshef, "When the Prime Minister was descending the last step, I saw someone on the right lift his hand, and start shooting."

Fact: Rabin was not on the steps, he was almost beside the car, three meters away, when he was shot. Amir would not have had the room to shoot him had Rabin still been descending the steps.

Nonetheless, as we shall soon see, *Maariv* also adopted this scenario early in the cover-up.

Damti: The shooter shouted, "It's nothing, they're not real bullets, they're blanks, this wasn't real."

Fact: Quite a mouthful to shout while in the midst of shooting someone. Amir denies shouting anything, and almost all witnesses heard similar shouts from the bodyguards.

Damti: "The truth is that I, myself, believed that it was like that, that it wasn't real. Nonetheless, I did what they taught me. I jumped behind the steering wheel.

Fact: The Kempler film shows indisputably that Damti did not immediately jump inside the car, rather he stayed outside and played some role in putting Rabin in the vehicle.

Damti: "After 20 or 30 meters of driving, I asked the Prime Minister, 'Are you hurt?' He answered, 'Yes.' Then I knew it was real and went into action. I asked him, 'Where does it hurt?' He answered, 'Ay, ay, it hurts in the back, but not terribly.' Then I speeded up."

Fact: What we are asked to believe is that Damti was taking a leisurely cruise until he had a conversation with Rabin which finally convinced him to speed up the trip. One of the many suspensions of disbelief required to buy this story is the fact that Yoram Rubin told almost the exact story to the *New York Times* on November 8, 1995, only this time Rabin told HIM he wasn't hurt badly. Unless they took turns asking Rabin the same questions, one or both are engaged in rather blatant falsehoods.

Damti: "Suddenly there was a barricade in the street. There were policemen manning it. The bodyguard [Rubin] shouted, 'Go, go,' but I stopped briefly and asked one of the policemen to guide me to the hospital."

We now examine what Damti told the Shamgar Commission.

Damti: "The Prime Minister descended the steps and arrived to within half a meter of his armoured limousine. I opened the door for Mrs. Rabin, then I heard a blast."

Fact: Damti has changed his story. No longer is Rabin on the last step, he is beside the car. But he just can't handle the complications of learning this new version. This time he opens the door for Leah Rabin, who in reality was on the steps, nine meters away.

Damti: "I drove away in a hurry. I was going to take Shaul Hamelekh Street [which is nowhere near, he must mean David Hamelekh Street, BC] but there were too many people. I wanted to take a short cut through Bloch Street, but there was a police barrier there and I thought the whole street was barricaded. I told the bodyguard all the streets were blocked and he suggested I pick up a policeman to guide us. For some reason, I received no communications *en route,* as was usually the case. I pushed down on the gas, and despite the delay, arrived at the hospital in a minute and a half."

Fact: Where to begin? Gone is Damti's moving conversation with Rabin. Instead Damti rushes to Bloch Street and sees a police barrier. This is actually what he should have been looking for, since the barriers were there to close the street to unauthorized traffic and speed the officials through. Instead, he became worried that the whole street was barricaded. In his previous story to Rafi Reshef, he was more than happy to see the police barricade, and despite protests from Rubin, he stopped and took in a policeman to direct him to the hospital. In this version to the Shamgar Commission the opposite happened; he didn't want to stop at the barrier, but Rubin suggested bringing in a policeman. And despite the delay, he arrived at the hospital in a minute and a half, seven minutes before the earliest report of his arrival by anyone else.

Why did the Shamgar Commission let him get away with all this perfidy and contradiction? And why wasn't Damti forced to finally explain why a 700 meter trip to the hospital really took over eight minutes to complete?

Was It Disinformation Or Was There A Shot From The Front?

From the beginning, I couldn't believe the sketch. The morning of the murder, *Maariv* reconstructed the event in a sketch made by Eldad Zakobitz. The assassin was standing on the sidewalk across the way from Rabin's car, and was shooting at Rabin's chest from the front, from a distance of about three meters.

The sketch accompanied the eyewitness report of journalist Yoav Limor:

> Then it happened. The terrible moment which I will never forget in my life. Suddenly I heard a shot, then another, then another. I stood a meter, perhaps two behind the Prime Minister with Aliza Goren ... They took the gun away from the youth who stood on the opposite sidewalk at a distance of five or six meters from the Prime Minister ... A minute after, a police officer said it was a blank gun and nothing happened to Rabin.

The next day, *Maariv* featured a full page sketch by Zakobitz. This time the assassin stood against the wall opposite the stairs and shot Rabin from a good three meters away, but behind him.

My first instinct was that this must be disinformation. My phone conversation with the artist seemed to confirm the suspicion.

BC: Why did you originally draw the sketch of the assassin shooting from the front?

Zakobitz: I was working with the information we had, and it turned out to be wrong. The next day I drew it correctly.

BC: Actually, your sketch is a very accurate depiction of what Yoav Limor wrote. I can understand the error if he was mistaken. But the next day's sketch was not right. You have the shooter firing from three meters away beside the steps.

Zakobitz: That's what everyone thought had happened. The facts weren't clear yet.

BC: Dozens of people had reported that Amir shot Rabin from a meter away by the next day. Yours is the only re-creation having him shoot from three meter's distance.

Zakobitz: I hope you're not writing that this was a Shabak murder.

BC: That's the way the evidence is pointing.

Zakobitz: Nonsense. There is a right and left wing in this country and the left doesn't kill. Only the right does. Rabin was killed by a religious zealot.

BC: I have hospital reports...

Zakobitz: Hospitals all lie. I was in one and they scribbled garbage.

BC: And I have police reports...

Zakobitz: They lie too. Rabin was murdered by the right and no one else.

My conversation with Yoav Limor was more dignified.

BC: You wrote that you were standing a meter or two behind Rabin when he was shot.
Limor: Yes, there's a photo which proves it.
BC: Then you must have been right beside Yigal Amir?
Limor: I was told he was just in front of me.
BC: So how could you think the shots came from six meters away in front of Rabin?
Limor: First of all, the distance wasn't six meters. I went back there and measured, and there is only three meters from where the shots actually came from, and where I thought they came from.
BC: Still, three meters is a big difference from where you were standing, maybe less than a meter from Amir. Could you really have made that kind of mistake?
Limor: I must have, obviously. I really am not familiar with weapons and there was a lot of hysteria at the time.
BC: You don't have to be an expert to hear a noise. I'd hate to drive with you if that's how you judge distances. Look, what if I told you, you might have been right. I have solid medical proof that Rabin suffered a frontal chest wound. Maybe, you did hear the fatal shot correctly.
Limor: What kind of proof?
BC: The first Ichilov surgeon's report, recorded statements by Ephraim Sneh and Gabi Barabash. They also report a frontal wound.

Is There More To The Feeling
Than Meets The Eye?

One of the questions I am often asked is if I think the organizers of the rally, Chich Lahat and Jean Freidman, were involved in the conspiracy. I reply that I don't know, but they sure had strange roles in the peace process.

Lahat was the Likud mayor of Tel Aviv, yet once Rabin announced his "peace" with the PLO, Lahat more than jumped on the opposition bandwagon. He organized a group of former IDF generals as a pro-peace lobbying group, and was apparently rewarded with an executive position on Jean Freidman's Ifshar Fund.

Freidman is a French television mogul closely connected to Shimon Peres. He spent $6 million of his own money to fund a massive public relations campaign on behalf of the peace agreements. Tens of thousands of road signs and wall posters flooded the country reading, "We Want Peace." Each and every one of them was victimized by grafitti artists who added only one word to the message, "We Want Another Peace."

Freidman founded the Ifshar Fund, supposedly to finance economic projects, but it was in reality, just another push "peace" idea. Lahat was his partner in the undertaking. Freidman financed and Lahat arranged the permits and municipal details for the rally where Rabin was murdered.

Yediot Ahronot reported, "Jean Freidman will not be interviewed for his reaction to Rabin's death. 'I have such feelings of guilt, I can't sleep,' he explained."

The same newspaper garnered a quote from Lahat while he was visiting the Rabin family. He said, "I came to shake hands with the family. I didn't say a word, didn't cry. For days I've been crying. I have irrational feelings of guilt."

What Were Amir's Intelligence Ties?

We discover in the clippings, that the internal Shabak investigation of the assassination revealed that one of Avishai Raviv's tasks was to recruit Yigal Amir into the service of the Shabak, but he was tested and found unsuitable.

We also learn from Gabi Bron, *Yediot Ahronot's* Knesset reporter, that, "As an employee of the Liaison Office, he was trained at a security course in shooting and weaponry. In one class he was trained in personal security. The teachers informed the class that the weakest points in an assassination are when the victim enters or leaves a car." A lesson he never forgot?

Who Was That Bearded Man?

Police Officers Sergei and Boaz Haran testified at the Shamgar Commission that they saw Amir talking with a bearded man in a black t-shirt minutes before the shooting. The officers added that it appeared they were acquainted with each other.

At Amir's hearing, *Yediot Ahronot* correspondent Booky Naeh reported, "The murderer of the Prime Minister, Yigal Amir held an impromptu press conference in the hall of the courthouse. Amir would not answer the question of who the bearded man was who spoke to him minutes before the murder. The existence of the man had been established by the commission of inquiry.

How Did The Information Leak So Quickly?

On the assassination night, Israel television reported that Amir tried to kill Rabin on two other occasions. Many, including myself, consider this fact erroneous. First, because it was reported too quickly. And second, because at his trial, Amir (who never shied from taking responsibility) vigorously denied that there was any previous assassination attempt.

The day after the assassination, *Maariv's* headline read: "The Assassin Also Planned To Murder Peres." This was not only denied by Amir, but was logistically imposssible even for Jesse James.

So why the false leaks, reportedly from the police interrogation?

Was There A Third Shamgar Murder Cover-up?

Not everyone was terribly happy that Meir Shamgar was appointed to head the commission of inquiry into the assassination. Michal Goldberg of *Yediot Ahronot* reported; "The three judges cut short their afternoon session to hear the claims of former police officer Yitzhak Keren who was protesting outside the building.

"I demand that you step down," Keren told Shamgar, 'It was during your tenure as the government legal adviser that you covered up the truth behind the murder of the soldier, Rachel Heller.'" Shamgar listened but did not react.

What Was Peres Trying To Say?

Shimon Peres's eulogy at Rabin's funeral contained a most intriguing passage. "Last Saturday," he said, "as we crossed arms, he told me that there was a high alert for an assassination attempt at this huge rally. We didn't know who would do it, nor did we expect the damage to be so great."

Peres seemed to have told the world that Rabin and he both knew about the coming assassination attempt at the rally, but weren't told who would try it. Neither did they expect it to be fatal.

Thirty days later, as many people pointed out to me, Peres, speaking at a memorial service to Rabin, said, "The bullets that pierced your chest did not cut down the fruits of your labor." Ignoring the inappropriate metaphor, at that time the bullets were commonly known to have pierced his back.

What Was Eitan Haber's Role In All This?

As mystifying as Peres's eulogy was, none compares to Eitan Haber's for pure surrealism. For those who have forgotten the tiny details of this drama, Eitan Haber was Rabin's director of the Defense Ministry Office. He went into Ichilov Hospital on the night of the murder and left with Rabin's bloody song sheet in hand. He announced the Prime Minister's death to the nation, then ran to Rabin's Defense Ministry Office and removed files from the cabinets. If that didn't appear suspicious enough, Haber mounted a personal vendetta against the Amir family, appearing at every court session during Yigal Amir's trial, and endlessly called the Amirs a family of monsters.

Without a doubt, I receive more correspondence about the round, black spot in the song sheet than any other clue. No one can properly explain it, but dozens of people have given it their best, if I may, shot.

One correspondent, Raanan Bavli sent me a copy of Haber's eulogy with the following comments: "This is getting interesting. I found a quote on the Internet from Chief Rabbi Lau who said that the song sheet was given to Leah Rabin at the hospital. However, no one but Peres has ever said the sheet had a hole in it. Also, the tapes show Rabin didn't even have his own copy."

This is pretty typical of the intelligent, inquiring correspondence I receive. So, let us try and figure out what it is about this song sheet that ignites so much interest.

First, a look at Haber's eulogy. He said, "Five minutes before you were shot, you sang from the sheet they gave you, so you could, as you always did, mouth the words. You had a thousand gifts and advantages, but singing wasn't counted among them. You bluffed your way through the song and after, as always, you folded the sheet into four even sections and put it in your jacket pocket. At the hospital, they gave me the sheet, still folded into four even sections. I would have liked to read from the sheet, but it's difficult. Your blood covers the printed words. Your blood is on 'The Song Of Peace.' This blood was drawn from you in your last moments of life to cover this sheet. Yitzhak, we miss you already."

It sounds like he misses the song sheet more. Almost his whole euology was about the sheet. As for Rabin, we learn he was fastidious about folding paper and couldn't sing very well. So what was the overwhelming interest Haber had in this piece of paper. Clues are given in his account which appeared in *Yediot Ahronot* on November 6, 1995.

Haber was waiting for Rabin to show up at a party when word of the shooting reached him. "I jumped into the car and drove like a madman, arriving at the hospital within minutes. I ran toward the operating rooms. I didn't know where I was going or how to get there. On the way, I saw his blood-soaked belongings and collected them."

Hospitals don't allow visitors anywhere near the operating rooms, yet Haber could just run, without knowing where he was going, into the operating area, and grab Rabin's blood-soaked belongings from the floor. Needless to say, Haber had no right to touch evidence, let alone handle and collect it.

"I knew something was wrong as soon as I entered the hospital and saw the driver, Menachem Damti. Someone said it was all over, but our hopes rose when his blood pressure returned to 90. Leah Rabin arrived, but I kept the bad news from her. By and by, I made notes for the reporters and phoned the American Ambassador to inform the White House that Rabin was shot. Someone had to do it."

But why Haber who was not a cabinet minister or even a Knesset member? Why would a lowly office director be the one to inform the White House of the shooting? This was in breech of diplomatic custom.

No where in Haber's account is there one mention of the song sheet. No one in the hospital gives it to him. As he tells it, he just picked it up off the floor and took it along with the other blood-soaked belongings. Why didn't he turn them over to the police? Why was he holding onto this sheet at Rabin's funeral, instead of it being held as state's evidence in the police forensics laboratory? What other belongings did he take away before the police could examine them? Who authorized him to gather them up? What was he doing in the operating area in the first place? And busy as he was gathering Rabin's belongings, calling the American ambassador, and preparing a press statement, he was too busy to tell Leah Rabin the truth.

Chapter Twenty Two
THE CULPRITS

The assassination of Yitzhak Rabin is a solvable crime. The answer lies not in Tel Aviv, but in Hebron. There, in March 1994, another horrid crime was perpetrated. Twenty-nine Arabs were slaughtered in the Cave of the Patriarchs. A commission of inquiry was set up to get to the truth. It was led by the former chief justice of the Israeli Supreme Court, Meir Shamgar, who would later head the commission of inquiry into Rabin's death.

Immediately following the massacre, an Arab reporter for the weekly news magazine *Yerushalaim* visited 25 survivors, including children, in six separate hospitals. One after another, they reported that the man accused of the crime, Baruch Goldstein, had at least one, perhaps two accomplices.

A dozen of these survivors testified to the Shamgar Commission that they saw an accomplice handing the shooter bullet clips as his ran out. And like the Rabin murder, strangely, nine of the soldiers who were supposed to guard the shrine were not on duty that morning. The three that were there testified that they saw Goldstein enter, followed a few minutes later by a civilian carrying a Galil assault weapon.

Shamgar ruled that Goldstein acted alone, that the soldiers who saw someone else follow him were mistaken, and that all the Arab witnesses perjured themselves. The implication of his verdict was that Arabs lie and their testimony was worthless. No honest court in the world would have reached Shamgar's conclusion.

Like his later commission into Rabin's murder, what was most striking was who didn't testify and what evidence wasn't admitted. The division of the General Security Services (Shabak) called the Non-Arab Anti-Subversive Unit, known as the Jewish Department, had agents planted throughout the territories, supposedly to surveil "radical" Jews and restrict their activities. The massacre was a notable failure, yet the head of the unit, Carmi Gillon, was not called to testify at the Shamgar Commission. Perhaps this was because his brother, Ilan Gillon, was the registrar of the commission responsible for organizing testimony.

Goldstein told friends of the upcoming slaughter. One friend was Shmuel Cytryn, later arrested without charge and imprisoned for months.* Goldstein told him that two days before the event that he received notice from the army "to prepare for a massacre."

Goldstein didn't survive the massacre and no one knows to this day how he died. No autopsy was ordered and the circumstances of his demise remain unknown.

After the Shangar whitewash, Gillon was named head of the Shabak, a strange reward in the aftermath of the Hebron fiasco. Or perhaps it wasn't such a fiasco after all. What is known for certain is that the unit continued to incite and entrap those territorial Jewish residents who opposed the Rabin peace process. The most publicized case is of the previously discussed Kahalani brothers serving 12 years for attempted murder of Arabs.**

And then of course, there is also the saga of the provocateur and conspirator, Shabak agent Champagne—Avishai Raviv. Legions of people heard Raviv publicly goading Amir into assassinating Rabin. These witnesses include four teenage girls, pupils of seminary teacher Sarah Eliash, who witnessed Raviv prodding Amir to kill Rabin, calling him a coward and a fake hero. This testimony was heard by the Shamgar Commission and was not included in the publicly released conclusions.

Raviv was no minor player. It was he who had posters of Rabin dressed in a Gestapo uniform printed and distributed at a large rally; it was he who organized the broadcast on Israel television's Channel One a month and a half before Rabin's assassination, of so-called Eyal members vowing to kill anyone who betrayed the land of Israel; it was he who orchestrated the performance, telling them what to say and where to stand.

Replacing Gillon as head of the anti-subversive unit was agent Kheshin, in turn appointed agent Eli Barak as his deputy. To this day very little is publicly known about Kheshin, even his first name. But Barak is a different matter. The week after Rabin's murder, the widely circulated newspaper *Kol Ha'ir,* without naming him, accused him of being responsible for the assassination.

Barak is a convicted drunk driver, known wife swapper and publicized stalker. After a near fatal accident caused by his intoxication, he lied to the police denying responsibility. His friend, and fellow wife swapper, died in mysterious circumstances. And in the most publicized incident of all, he terrorized and stalked a radio reporter, Carmela Menashe. Instead of firing this security hazard, Rabin sent him abroad on a assignment and later approved his appointment in Hebron.

In the most obvious cover-up of the Shamgar Commission, seven Shabak agents and officers involved in the "snafu" that led to Rabin's death, including Kheshin, received notices that they were liable for criminal prosecution. Barak did not. Kheshin was later exonerated by the commission despite being in charge of the Raviv operation. But Barak, who was apparently Raviv's immediate superior, wasn't even called to testify in open court.

A few persistent reporters tried tracking Barak down at his home in Kochav Yair, but were rudely turned away by Shabak officers surrounding his block. The key to uncovering the truth clearly lies with Eli Barak, but he has been protected by the government. And because of this glaring cover-up of his activities, not a few people have speculated, probably wrongly, that he was the mystery man who closed the back door of Rabin's car from the inside, before the "wounded" Rabin entered the back seat.

In February of 1996, the Jerusalem correspondent for the *London Observor,* Shay Batia, reported that he spoke with two Shabak agents fired since the assassination. They informed him that Amir was supposed to fire blanks and that Rabin's chief security aide Danny Yatom was involved in the preparations for the scam. His silence, purchased when appointed chief of the Mossad, is eerily reminiscent of Carmi Gillon's rise to head of the Shabak after the Hebron massacre.

Of Gillon, it is well known that he was a far leftist who despised the settlers and was heard refering to them as "neo-nazis." His attitude was revealed in his 1991 Masters thesis completed at Haifa Unversity which analysed the settler movement from a perspective of hatred.

Two days before the assassination, Gillon flew to Paris, despite pleas from subordinates not to leave before the rally, in light of the national mood. A joke that made the rounds after the assassination has Gillon calling Leah Rabin on the night of the murder and offering his deep condolences. She asks him, "What for?" "Oops," he said, "I forgot about the time difference."

EPILOGUE

There they are, stacked on a chair beside me, dozens of pages of publications claiming to know who gave the order to murder Rabin. The *New American* calls his demise a "CFR" (Council On Foreign Relations) murder. The *Japanese Times* article says Rabin was caught up in a financial scam over stolen software called PROMIS and the same folks who killed Clinton aide Vince Foster, assassinated him. *Conspiracy Nation* presents a view that the Vatican financed the operation. From the Internet are accusations that 32nd degree Mason Rabin was knocked off for revealing cult secrets. Then there are the Israelis who tell me Peres was behind the hit because he had the most to gain.

I am not dismissing any of the possibilities and my original intention was to list them all and judge their relative merits. In fact, I wrote 30 pages of a final chapter before deciding that it would be self-defeating for me to engage in speculation when the rest of the book is backed up by powerful evidence.

I don't know who gave the order, but there is a clearcut trend amongst those trying to figure out who did: Rabin was murdered by outside forces. I think this supposition may eventually be proven true. Two months before he was murdered, Rabin began spilling the beans about who was really behind the peace process. He told *ABC News* and then William Safire of the *New York Times* that the peace process was forced on him by George Bush at a meeting in Kennebunkport, Maine, in September, 1992. According to Rabin,

Bush told him to "prepare the Israeli public for some painful with-drawals."

He returned to Israel and appeared on a friendly television inter-view. He jokingly told startled viewers that "Netanyahu phoned Kissinger and asked him to issue a proclamation condemning the placement of American soldiers on the Golan Heights. Henry called me back laughing. He said he told Netanyahu to stop bothering him."

It's not that funny a story. Rabin was saying that both his and Netanyahu's diplomacy had to be approved by Kissinger. To those familiar with modern conspiracy theory, Rabin's ties with Council On Foreign Relations executives Bush and Kissinger are most sinister.

In March, 1997, *Haaretz* provided a motive for Rabin's murder in two front page articles. Rabin's last meeting with Clinton was explosive. It seems Rabin had hypothetically asked Secretary of State Warren Christopher how Syrian President Assad would react to a withdrawal from the Golan Heights right to the shores of the Sea of Galilee. Christopher informed Assad that Rabin was prepared to withdraw to the shoreline. According to *Haaretz,* "Rabin let loose a vicious flow of invective against Christopher and Middle East envoy, Dennis Ross..." Not a very wise thing to do against two prominent CFR members.

So far, the theory that Rabin was murdered to keep him quiet seems the most likely. Needless to say, he was worth more dead than alive to someone in a position of extraordinary power.

That the murder was planned in Israel is less likely to me. There are only a handful of people with the power and influence within intelligence circles to issue an assassination order, and all are allied to foreign decision makers. It seems highly unlikely that any of them would act independently to eliminate Rabin. To do so would have meant facing the wrath of Rabin's powerful backers. The order had to have come from beyond Peres, Sharon, Shamir or whoever could have theoretically organized the crime.

If the foreign hit theory seems far-fetched, consider some of the alternatives gaining cliques of advocates.

First, there is the mystical theory, that the murder was an ordained spiritual act. The advocates have some intriguing evidence, including the internationally publicized Bible Code revelation pre-dicting Rabin's murder and even naming Amir. More proof is offered in the activities of a Russian-born follower of the late Rabbi Meir Kahane, Avigdor Askin, who worked at the Mossad's Soviet desk between 1978–85. He held a public ceremony a month before the assassination in which he read an ancient Jewish death curse, the *pulsa dinara,* against Rabin. Rabin was murdered five years to the week of Kahane.

Far spookier is the fact that the Torah reading for the week of the assassination included the sentence, "Shoot, shoot bad Rabin," in consecutive letters. Then there is the indisputable fact that Yigal Amir's name began and ended with a Y and R, in both English and Hebrew, Yitzhak Rabin's initials. Subtract these letters and Amir's name in Hebrew becomes Salvation Of The People.

In 1996, a book of fiction was published in Israel in Russian whose story has Rabin surviving the shots, being replaced by another victim and flying to Hong Kong for a permanent retirement. Those who consider the book prophetic note that Kissinger was in Hong Kong when the assassination took place, and didn't come to the funeral, explaining feebly that he couldn't get a flight out.

Every time I lecture, someone in the audience expounds on the body-switch theory. A most unlikely advocate of the concept is Israel's leading conspiracy writer Joel Bainerman, author of a scathing book about the covert, illegal agendas of the Bush administration (*Crimes Of A President,* SPI Books, New York, 1992).

I choose to ignore all these outlandish explanations and concentrate on the indisputable facts. Most outstanding among them are the police and medical documents which prove Rabin was shot pointblank and in the chest, neither of which Yigal Amir could possible have done. So if Yigal Amir couldn't have done the deed, who then murdered Yitzhak Rabin?

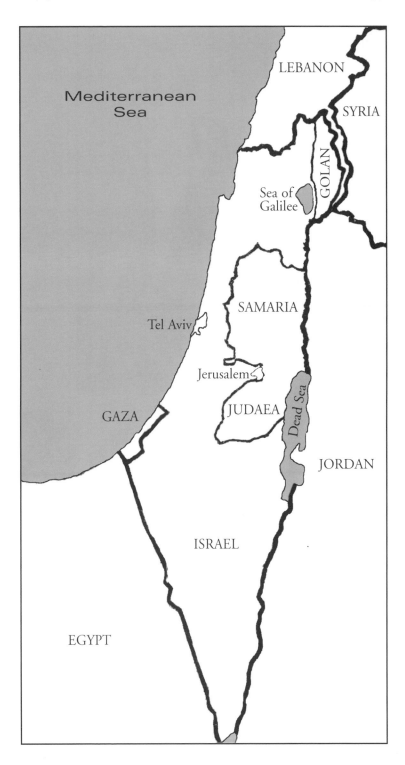

Avishai Raviv's
Rabin-as-SS-officer poster.

Avishai Raviv in typical repose.

Police take Amir's ID one month before the murder, at a demonstration outside the home of Knesset member Alex Goldfarb.

Yidal Amir at a hunger strike, April, 1994, Bar Ilan campus.

Avishai Raviv holds suspected murder weapon of Rabin. On his t-shirt is a picture of Rabin and the caption: No Rest for Traitors.

Rabin with his
longtime friend
Meir Shamgar.

Shabak Chief Carmi Gillon

Rabin with
Yorum Rubin,
behind.

Rabin with song
sheet minutes before
shooting is heard.

Song sheet after.

Before the murder, well-protected Shimon Peres passes by Amir (1).
Notice the ski mask and glasses drawn on faces of bodyguards.
If only for reasons of security, the film was tampered with.

This photo of
Rabin being
pushed into
the car, clearly
disproves
Yorum Rubin's
testimony that
Rabin jumped
into the car.

The doctored Kempler film still from *Yediot Achronot* front's page photo: 1. Rabin 2. Amir 3. Mordi Yisrael 4. Damti, driver 5. Yorum Rubin Notice that the right handed Amir appears to be shooting with his left.

Standard procedure. Rabin's back is securely protected by a bodyguard. This photo taken less than two months before the murder.

Rabin's bodyguard, Yoram Rubin

Avishai Raviv, the intelligence operative codenamed "Champagne," was arrested after the murder and released within a few hours.

Shamgar Commission judges, from left: Tzui Zamir, Meir Shamgar and Ariel Rosen Tzui

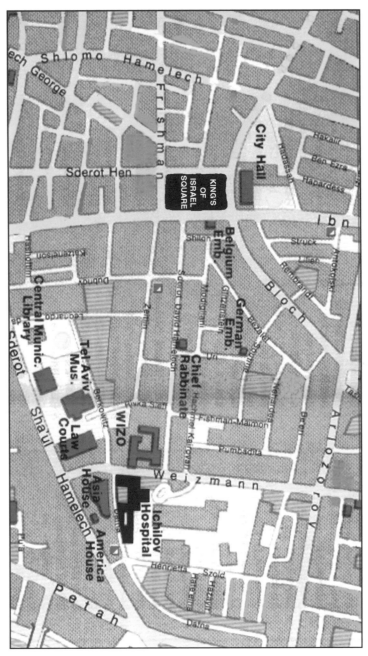

A street map of Tel Aviv clearly shows direct routes from
King of Israel Square to Ichilov Hospital.

Recontruction of the murder.

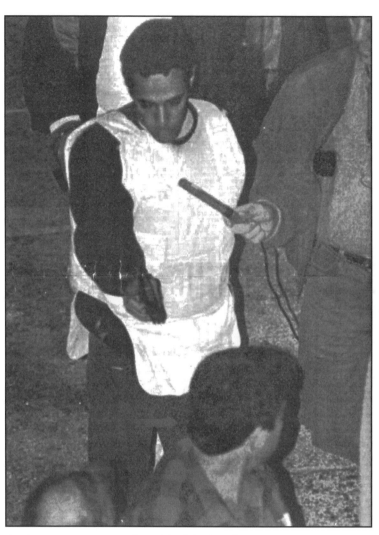

Amir reconstructs murder with right hand.

Eitan Haber holds the song sheet at the funeral.

פרס: 54%
ביבי: 23%

עבודה: 46 מנדטים, ליכוד – 30,
מרץ – 8, צומת – 6, מולדת – 2

אילו נערכו הבחירות לראשות הממשלה
היום, והמתמודדים היו שמעון פרס ובנימין
נתניהו – עבור מי היית מצביע/ה?

לא השיבו	לא החליטו	לא יצביעו	נתניהו	פרס
1%	10%	12%	23%	54%

אילו נערכו הבחירות לכנסת היום –
עבור איזו רשימה היית מצביע/ה?

מנדטים בכנסת	תחזית המנדטים	הרשימה הנוכחית
44	46	עבודה
32	30	ליכוד
12	8	מרץ
8	6	צומת
3	2	מולדת
6	6	מפד"ל
4	4	יהדות התורה
6	5	ש"ס
5	6	חד"ש, מד"ע
–	2	דוד לוי
–	3	הדרך השלישית
–	2	רשימת עולים
120	120	סה"כ

האם הממשלה צריכה או לא צריכה
להמשיך במימוש ההסכם עם הפלשתינים
כמותכנן?

לא השיבו	לא צריכה	צריכה
3%	23%	74%

האם אמונך בפעילות השב"כ נפגע או לא
נפגע?

לא השיבו	לא נפגע	נפגע
4%	50%	46%

הסקר נערך בימים ג' וד', בשבוע האבל על
מות רה"מ יצחק רבין ז"ל. השתתפו בו 501
מרואיינים, המהווים מידגם מייצג של כלל
האוכלוסיה הבוגרת במדינה. טעות הדגימה
המירבית – 4%.

The day of the assassination Netanyahu lead Rabin in the polls 56% to 32%. Five days after the poll is Peres 54%, Netanyahu 23%.